A PLACE OF GRACE

Marylyn I. Butkovic

Acknowledgements

Thanks to my mom, sisters and brother for sticking by me through the years, taking me in and loving me so well. Thanks to Susan Cravey for editing this book, asking probing questions and making the story flow. I would have given up long ago without her encouragement and input.

To my children, I love you all deeply though it must have seemed at times that I was distant. I apologize for the wasted years.

A Place of Grace

Table of Contents

Chapter One
A Normal Life

Even after all these years, a knot of breath-robbing panic forms in my gut when I wonder all over again what on earth I was thinking to get into such a fix. Whenever that night in the New Mexico blizzard comes to mind, that's what happens to me. The five of us were headed north to Flagstaff with plans to go through Gallup and then on to Albuquerque. It all seemed so straightforward.

But there we were in the midst of a snowstorm and we pulled over to wait it out. The cold was soul-piercing and there was so much snow on the ground that we couldn't even get a fire started. The truck's heater was useless, as if we had enough gas to keep it running anyway. We bundled up as best we could with every blanket we had with us to keep ourselves and the children warm. But it wasn't going very well.

Then out of nowhere, Tommy Lee appeared. A local Navajo man, he led us to his home where he gave us a warm fire, good food and a safe place to sleep. I have no doubt he saved all of our lives that night, especially that of tiny, newborn Lavina. Tommy welcomed us to stay as long as we wanted. He made it comfortable for us and we

5

happily stayed for the next year and a half. This memory also reminds me of something else.

One day, I realized this story was a picture of my entire adult life. Always headed somewhere else, always on to the next thing, always following the wrong path, always dancing with some kind of danger, and always facing an ugly downfall, children and all. Over and over again. But finally, a savior shows up out of nowhere, providing warmth, safety and love.

My life started out quite normally. I was one of six children in an Italian, Catholic family in Cleveland, Ohio. We were a happy family, living in the suburbs. Dad worked as a foreman for an electrical contractor, and our mother was a stay-at-home wife and homemaker. Life didn't get much more normal.

Normal that is, until 1961. I was 14 and my father died. I can't imagine any young girl is ready to be without a loving father, and I definitely wasn't. I needed him. My mother needed him. We all needed him. Boom. Almost overnight we went from really normal to really needy, but my mother rose to the challenge.

She went to work part-time with our family doctor. She then learned to drive and began working full-time in the school cafeteria, and later, for a local Sears & Roebuck store where she retired at the

6

age of seventy-five. She remained a strong anchor in all our lives for the rest of her days. She was our place of grace.

My drift began on Prom Night in 1965. I had broken up with my longtime boyfriend a month earlier and since I didn't have a date for the dance, I went to a bar. I met Andy that night, a college student, and we began to date. He introduced me to his friend Nick, a guy in his thirties. He seemed to know so much about life and had even travelled all over the world. He fascinated me.

Nick and I became friends and soon began to date. Andy just sort of faded into the background as things got pretty hot and heavy between me and Nick. By 1965 standards, I'd say Nick and I were lovers. We didn't sleep together – good Catholic girls didn't do that then – but we did everything else we could think of! After a while, that romance faded, too. I dated plenty of other guys once that was over, but no one I particularly liked.

Then I met Skip, at the same bar where I'd met Andy. He spotted me, pursued me, and I let myself be caught and swept away all the way to the altar. That's what good girls were expected to do in 1965 – get married. It didn't hurt that Donna, my good friend from high school, had just gotten married and I thought she was cool which made getting married cool, too. Moreover, I had nothing else to do at the time, Skip was different and actually liked me, so why not. It all added up to a match made in heaven, for sure.

Our courtship was short – we were married within six months of the night we met. It was also rocky. Technically, I had remained a virgin so far and probably had it somewhere in the back of my mind that I would remain so until our wedding night. Not that there weren't plenty of hot and heavy make-out sessions.

Problem was, it became more and more clear to me I just wasn't ready for marriage. I tried to explain it to Skip one winter night while we were out driving around; I even tried to give him back the ring. Boy, did that backfire. He got very angry, driving like a madman through an icy parking lot. He was a mechanic and race car driver, not to mention an ex-Marine, and knew exactly what he was doing. He made the car spin and skid recklessly, until he scared the hell out of me and I took back what I'd said about not marrying him.

The rest of the evening went about as well the first part of the evening. We were in the basement making out and it got further and further along – well beyond what I was comfortable with. I was scared and resisted and terrified my mother would hear what was going on. So, I just gave in. Not a very lovely first time. I sometimes wonder if, by today's standards, it would have been considered rape. Clearly, I didn't know how to say no.

Secretly, I had long fantasized about some knight in shining armor coming along to rescue me. I was still looking for that fantasy savior just before Skip and I walked down the aisle. We were married in July, 1966.

Things between us remained pleasant for the most part, then after about 3 years, I became very discontent. I had a miscarriage, which I figured was my own fault because I knew I wasn't ready for children. And I was not at all sure I even wanted to stay married. I explored ideas ranging from the reasonable, such as going to college, to the insane, like running far, far away. I even regretted not staying with my first love from high school. So, instead I had an affair with my old boyfriend Andy. When Skip found out, he came very close to shooting us. So much for happily ever after.

I wanted a divorce, but Skip didn't. He did everything he could to keep his bride. In return, I did everything I could to hurt him. I had more affairs. I was very unhappy and unable to figure out what I wanted from life. I was still looking for that knight in shining armor. A savior. Ultimately, I moved out and into my own apartment, and thanks to The Pill, did my part for the budding sexual revolution right up until the final divorce decree and well beyond.

My discontent showed itself in every part of my life. I changed jobs several times. I took some college courses but didn't stick with it. I wanted to travel and felt like being married was holding me down. After being a devout Catholic all my life, the events of the times and my own observations began to lead me away from the church. Too many man-made rules!

Although I did believe in God. The evening of the day my father died, I prayed for God to assure me that my daddy was with Him in heaven. I put my rosary, which had been broken in two for quite some time, under my pillow after praying. When I awoke, I hesitantly reached for the rosary and much to my astonishment it was in one piece! God made Himself very real to me that morning and I never stopped believing He was real. I never told anyone about it, not even my mother, until I finally told her before she passed away at the age of ninety-one.

As I got older and my discontent grew, I pushed God away and only brought Him out when I was scared or needed something. I now know that He made Himself real to me over and over again through the years and never pushed me away or let go of me.

My friend Donna's life had taken a fascinating turn. She was an artist, living in a communal home, smoking pot and tripping on psychedelics. I loved hanging out with her and her hippie friends – it was exciting and interesting. One of them suggested I read Generation of Vipers, written in 1942 by Phillip Wylie. It criticized various aspects of contemporary society including Christianity, politicians, doctors, etc. I read the Bible for myself for the first time. No one I knew in the Catholic Church ever read the Bible; we relied on the priests to tell us what it said. I began searching for something or someone I could believe in, something that would define the meaning of life for me.

My many relationships with men got complicated. I dated one guy for about two years, and when I realized he was about to ask me to marry him, I confessed my other boyfriends. He found out one of them was a black man, which repulsed him. The black man found out about the others, called me a whore and left. I had never thought of myself like that but wondered if maybe it was true.

My family knew nothing of my discontent or the secret life I was leading, and my younger brother and sisters actually looked up to me. I think that was the moment I realized I had to leave Cleveland; the fact that it was a big city didn't matter - it was closing in on me. It was 1969.

I decided to leave the town I had grown up in and head west. One of my girlfriends, Susan, and I bought an old Ohio Bell van, fixed it up, loaded up and then hit the road. Traveling with us were her two-year old daughter and a friend of ours named Jared. He needed a ride out west so we asked him to travel with us. Little did I realize that a life I could never have imagined lay ahead of me.

Never.

Chapter Two
Westward Bound

Susan and I had met Jared when partying with a lot of other potheads at a local college campus in Cleveland. He had a brother living in Golden, Colorado, just outside Denver, so that was our first destination. It was September and a snowstorm accompanied us to the top of the mountain to his brother's cabin.

Except for the snowstorm, everything in this part of the country was new to me. I had never seen a real mountain before and I immediately fell in love with it all – the air, the rocks, the trees, the stars. I ventured outside at night and looked at the mountains in awe. It felt as if you could touch God from there. It impressed me that I actually understood what John Denver meant when he sang Rocky Mountain High. I was so naïve!

The next day, the four of us continued our journey and arrived in Newport, Oregon, a few days later. Jared left us to hitchhike the rest of the way to San Francisco. Now it was the vast Pacific Ocean that captivated me. I had grown up next to Lake Erie, a beautiful body of water in its own right, but the ocean was breathtaking. We rented a little house right on the beach and each got a waitress job at one of the resorts in the area. We wanted to stay here for a while.

We began to build a social circle with the local hippies. I became good friends with Judy, who took me under her wing. She was the leader of a communal house in town. She introduced me to LSD and I dropped acid for the first time there.

I was given a combination of Orange Sunshine and Window Pane acid, she made sure I was really high. I was just nauseated at first; then, I realized everything I looked at was like seeing it for the first time. Furniture became animated, wood grain vibrated with life, pictures on the wall melted and the colors ran down the walls. People looked like beautiful gods and goddesses.

The person acting as my trip guide took me outside so I could experience everything, and because I felt like the walls were closing in on me. In the darkness the stars were magnificent, more brilliant and numerous than I'd ever seen before. I felt invisible and invincible. I was yelling at the top of my voice and had to be hushed because there were police nearby. Then I was escorted to the beach. The draw of the waves was so powerful I wanted to walk into the ocean. My guide led me elsewhere, thankfully. It was quite an experience. I definitely wasn't in Cleveland anymore!

Judy also introduced me to a man named Herk, short for Hercules. He was 30, divorced and a beatnik. Well, a wannabe beatnik since his only contact with that lifestyle was through books. His real name was Albert but because he was born prematurely and lived, his father nicknamed him Hercules.

Herk adored books, especially those by Jack Kerouac or Herman Hesse, or about World War II history, or art. Bearded and slightly pudgy, he had a way with words – and women. He had been in the army stationed in Germany. He and his former wife had two children.

Like many others, I was charmed by his sly smile and mischievous laugh. He was gregarious and enjoyed starting up conversations with random strangers. He called it "picking their brains". Many times, while sitting in Moe's, the local waterfront hangout, he would just go and sit down at a stranger's table and start talking. They loved it and it made him a local icon.

We began a relationship and soon I moved in with him and his Springer spaniel he named, Cerberus after the three-headed dog in Greek mythology who guarded the gates of hell. He lived in a little cabin overlooking Yaquina Bay. Herk called it The Chicken Roost. He was my first live-in boyfriend. Even with all of my boyfriend experience, I had never lived with a man I wasn't married to. I had come a long distance from Cleveland, for sure. And there was a lot more to come.

Herk had many friends and acquaintances in the area, and we entertained a lot. I delighted in the challenge of whipping up gourmet meals, making the most of The Chicken Roost's wood stove and hot plate. Herk nicknamed me Serena Serape because I always wore a colorful poncho. I was known as Serena until I returned to Ohio to stay three decades later.

We often tripped with all the hippies, and it was always fun. In fact, Herk and I were tripping when I conceived. I remember that night vividly. We went to the beach and built a bonfire. I can still see Herk running naked on the beach; in my mind then he had turned into a satyr. Both of us were also very drunk.

Of course, nothing is ever as idyllic as it seems. Always dancing with danger, remember? Herk never knew a stranger, but strangers are strangers, after all. One night, when I was about five months pregnant, Herk dragged home one of the drunken pseudo-intellectuals he'd met that day. I was already in bed. Herk passed out on the sofa and this stranger began to rape me. I yelled for help but Herk was dead to the world. I didn't know what to do; it all happened pretty fast. Afterwards, I ran into the bathroom, locked the door and waited for him to leave. I just wanted to

16

forget that it ever happened. I never told anyone about it. So much for peace, love and drugs.

Also, I knew Herk was seeing a former lover, a professor at Berkeley. In my previous life, I may have been bothered by this. Our free-love lifestyle had put all that to rest. So, while still pregnant, I had an affair of my own with Herk's friend Gary. Which suited Gary, because it was his revenge for Herk having slept with his long-time girlfriend. As Herk was often known to say, "What goes 'round, comes 'round."

Dick and Jane, a couple we became friends with, had recently given birth to a son. Both of them had graduated from college in Ann Arbor, Michigan, so Herk loved to pick their brains. Their choice of having a home birth fascinated me, so I read up on it and decided that was what I wanted, too. I asked around and found a midwife, a guy who had served in Vietnam as a medic. He agreed to trade his services for an old MG convertible that Herk owned and planned to restore someday.

About a month before I was due, Herk and I moved out of The Chicken Roost and into a house in the Nye Beach section of town we shared with Dick, Jane and baby Zack. One funny memory is the Halloween party Jane had. I was so huge by then and being only five-feet-tall I looked like I had swallowed a pumpkin. I donned a bright orange coat and costume done. What a sight!

Herk's drinking had been a vague concern to me for a while, but the closer it got for me to have the baby, the worse his drinking became. He was having an affair and throwing wild drinking and drug parties at home. One night, I snapped and kicked everyone out of the house. Looking back, it must have been the hormones, because I was usually much too meek to stand up for myself.

On a stormy November day, I went into labor. The midwife only lived 50 miles away but because of the storm and the dark, winding road it took him several hours to arrive. Jane had been coaching me in the birthing process and helped me through ten hours of labor. The whole neighborhood of hippies came over to see the birth. There were so many people in the room it was stifling; I felt they were sucking all the air from the room.

Jane and the midwife were a godsend but Herk was no help at all since he was passed out drunk in the next room. Our son, whom we named Rocky, weighed in at over nine pounds. Ouch! I nursed Rocky for the next two years and continued to use pot and LSD. Back then, we just plain didn't realize the effect this could have. As much as I hate to admit it, even if I had known, I was so wrapped up in my new lifestyle that I'm not sure I would have done any differently.

The following spring, we moved to a large ranch house on a country road, 10 miles inland from Beaver Creek, Oregon. We thought a logger must have built the house because five-foot logs fit into the furnace in the underground garage. Dick, Jane and Zach came to live with us – there was plenty of room! In the summer, my mother and sisters Peggy and Chris came to visit. They'd never been west of Detroit! One night, we had a cookout featuring a lingcod wrapped in foil and baked in the ground. Everyone raved about it. Everyone enjoyed their visit and I loved spending the time with them.

I had been experimenting a little with Zen and transcendental meditation – that was the in thing, after all. Some of my hippie girlfriends had also begun to delve into witchcraft. I somehow sensed this was not a good path, so I stayed away from it. But I sure did witness a lot of strange goings on, and none of it was very good.

I wasn't taken by the Gestalt workshops that were so popular in town. Since Herk was sleeping with the woman who was facilitating a workshop, she invited me to join one of the sessions. I gave it a try but didn't get much out of it. It was an interesting experience, but I was very uncomfortable with the touchy-feely emphasis and telling my inmost thoughts to a group of strangers was not my style.

I heard lots of rumors about what went on at the sessions late into the night. Orgies and such. Also, not my style. One night, the house where one of the sessions was being held burned down when candles were left burning all night. The woman who owned the house had been turned on by the local hippies and she completely changed her lifestyle from plain housewife to drugged out hippie almost overnight. She got close to the Gestalt folks and joined them in experimenting with different sex partners. It was during one of their trysts, the house burned down. Crazy times.

While Gestalt wasn't my thing, psychedelics were another story! I used them with total abandon. Once, when I was tripping on mescaline, something happened that should have made me think twice about using drugs and being a parent, but it didn't. It was a warm summer day and I decided to take a walk with Rocky in his backpack. As I started out, I ducked under the clothesline not realizing the rope had hooked around the baby's neck. Stoned and oblivious, I just kept walking. Finally, it stopped me up short and pulled me back. Miraculously, Rocky didn't have a mark on him. It took me a long time to realize what the consequences might have been, and even longer to admit that the drugs had anything to do with it.

Later that very same day, Herk was listening to music in the front room and playing with Rocky. I walked in to see what they were up to and, out of nowhere, Herk threw him to me from about 10 feet away. I caught him, but just barely. I couldn't figure out why he did that. Herk was drinking and tripping, of course.

While our drug use just seemed to go right over my head, I was having trouble with Herk's drinking, and the throwing incident didn't help my trust in him very much. I had thought about leaving him, but for whatever reason, we stayed together. Herk didn't complete the work he'd promised to do in lieu of some of the rent, so we got kicked out of the ranch house.

We rented and shared a two-story house in Newport with Dick and Jane. There was enough room for Jane and me to start making batik cloth in the basement. Jane had the expertise in fabric dying and she taught me the craft, I had learned to sew at an early age and made much of my own clothing. Eventually, we rented a small shop and sold our clothing and consignment items. But that didn't last very long.

Because Herk had slept with Jane, tensions grew between him and Dick. So, we moved out of town into a converted milk house that sat on 20 acres on the Siletz River. The property owners lived nearby and had a small campground they rented to weekend campers. In exchange for rent, we worked together to maintain a large garden. There was a recreational building at the campground that had a commercial kitchen. Our landlady took me under her wing and taught me to make donuts with the equipment. On weekend mornings, I made donuts to sell to the campers.

I also began raising goats and learned to milk and care for them. Boy, were they a pain! They kept getting loose and eating everything in sight, including the tasty garden produce. With the goat's milk, I also made yogurt and some cheese. While we had indoor plumbing and electricity, I did all the cooking on a wood cook stove. As far as I was concerned, this was paradise!

During our second year in the milk house, things got pretty rough between me and Herk. He quit his job at the local lumber mill, so I got a part-time job serving drinks at a pub. At Christmas, Herk worked at a tree farm, and also spent a lot of time getting drunk and sleeping around. I figured what was good for the gander was good for the goose, so I took on some lovers, too.

Needless to say, we fell apart and I finally left with Rocky. It was 1974. Rocky and I stayed with one of my girlfriends, affectionately named Hairy Mary. We lived in a little shack with no electricity or running water. It had a wood stove, which also served as the cook stove and water heater. I was primitive, but it was a free roof over our heads.

After a few encounters with local men who turned out to be either married or just plain nasty, I decided to return home to Ohio. But, something else came up and I didn't make it back there for another 30 years.

Remember? On to the next thing, dancing with danger, waiting for a savior to show up.

My story was just beginning.

Chapter Three
The Real Story Begins

I met John in a bar one night in April, and I slept with him that night. Both of us were swimming in Jack Daniels and riding high on pot. The next day, I went with him to see his place, which was located south of Newport, and that was that. I expected to never hear from him again.

Instead, he showed up at the shack the next day. We tripped on acid together and in the evening, I told him I loved him. Actually, it wouldn't have mattered who he was. He could have been a tree or a dog and I would have been in love; it's just an overwhelming feeling you get sometimes when you're high on acid.

John told me he loved me, too, and wanted me to come home with him and meet his wife. He explained he had always wanted two wives and to live off the land like Indians; we could make and sell handcrafts to support ourselves. It was beyond the Hippie lifestyle – it was other. It was immersing ourselves into the ancient American Indian culture. John had studied the culture, spent time among Native Americans and had decided to start his own tribe.

Talk about a savior! I thought this was just the best thing I'd ever heard. With Rocky in tow we went to meet his wife, Rachel. It was raining, as usual, and we had to wade through giant puddles to get to his so-called cabin. It was more of a one-room shack with an attached lean-to for John's horse, Tomahawk. John had cut an opening in the living area wall so the horse could put its head through. In my limited view of the world, it reminded me of the TV show Mr. Ed. That was the extent of my experience with horses, other than a trail ride in the park many years earlier.

What little I knew about horses was vast compared with what I knew about the lifestyle I was about to take on. The plan was to be nomadic, having a teepee we could set up wherever we were or making shelter out of whatever the land provided. I would join them in making Indian crafts, bartering for what we needed, and living off the grid.

All I knew was that I was fascinated with every aspect of the idea. The lean-to had no indoor plumbing, or even an outhouse nearby. We used the woods.

I had no idea what to expect when I met his wife. We didn't have much to say to each other. We both just went along with it because we were so enamored with John. He was very charismatic. She was Native American and had been with him for six years. John and I had known each other less than a week.

We soon formalized our arrangement in a unique ceremony. A very cold creek ran through the property – very cold! John and Rachel had constructed a stick-house-style sweat lodge next to it. We took some LSD, then fired up the sweat lodge until it was really hot. Inside, we passed around a pipe and sang Native American chants and prayers.

The next step was to run naked to the creek and dunk ourselves. John and Rachel did this without hesitation. Knowing how cold the water was, I definitely hesitated and was then bombarded with insults about how weak and cowardly I was. Even two-year old Rocky was included in the ceremony. Our dream had begun.

Not long after that, the property where we were living was sold and we were asked to leave. We needed food and money and transportation to do that, so I applied for food stamps and welfare. I lied about the number of people in my household to try to get more than I was really due. I had to make an appointment to meet with a social worker at the cabin to verify my living circumstances. I had to hurriedly make it look like we were still living there. What a fiasco! The social worker didn't believe me.

Where I got the idea – or the guts – to do such a thing, I don't know. I'd never done anything like it before. I could have been charged with welfare fraud. Looking back, I now figure it was the grace of God that I only got denied assistance. Better that than prison. We didn't stick around long enough to find out if they were going to come after me. The agencies weren't as savvy then as they are now, but we had to get out of town all the same.

We still needed money. While we figured that out, we stayed on a friend's property. Next, I came up with the idea of writing some bad checks from my bank account. At least I think it was my idea. At this point I was so enamored with John and what we were doing that I wasn't thinking about anything else. Somewhere deep inside I guess I was ashamed because I never told anyone about it, especially my mother or my family. Already I was well into living the absolute opposite of all they valued and the way I was raised.

After all, we were not only against the social norms, we were anti-government, believing the government owed Native Americans. Rachel and her family were involved with the American Indian Movement; I was all in and was determined to help them get some of what was owed them.

For almost a week I got away with writing about $500 worth of bad checks. That, along with selling my pickup truck, got us enough money to leave town. We replaced the pickup with "Big Red", a 4-wheel drive International Harvester Scout. We took out the back seats and built a sleeping platform in the space. We packed all we owned underneath the platform or on the roof rack. We were ready for adventure!

But first, there was a confrontation with Herk. He didn't want me to take his son away, but he really had no choice in the matter. John ran him off with a gun. Later, we saw him in town. He tried once again to confront Rachel, but she hurled a brick and hit him in the head. He still bears scars from that assault.

With that, we left town in a hurry, knowing that the police were probably going to get involved.

Chapter 4
John & Rachel

At this point, I should give a little background on John and Rachel. They are both complicated people, and very different from one another. I don't think I've ever known anyone quite like either of them.

John, who was not American Indian but of Irish ancestry, was abandoned by his mother as a toddler. His father joined the navy, leaving John to be passed around between his great-grandparents, grandparents, and a great uncle. When he was about nine, his dad remarried and John went to live with him and his stepmother, Jean. She had no children of her own, and suddenly she was mother and caregiver to a very angry and sickly young boy.

John was plagued by a host of allergies and was often bedridden. He had an extreme allergic reaction to poison oak once and missed a lot of school. Jean took good care of him, but they argued often, especially as he got older. He hated his stepmother, so much so that at the very mention of her name he would become very angry. He often accused me of being like her because for whatever reason he thought we were both Capricorns.

Now I realize it was just another way for him to control me. I didn't find out until many years later that she had a late November birthdate, which made her a Sagittarius. We were big believers in astrology then. Not unusual for the 70's.

John quit high school a few months shy of graduation and left home. He had almost no further contact with his family until he was nearly 40 years old. In his mid-twenties, he contacted his birth mother who was living in Idaho with her new family. She came to see him in Oregon and he found out he had a half-sister. He never saw his mother again after that and they didn't stay in contact. Needless to say, John was left with some mother issues, and I came to believe he carried a deep hatred and distrust of women and needed to dominate and control them.

He got into drugs in his mid-teens, was arrested for selling, and spent time in Juvenile Detention and drug rehab programs. He met Rachel and her family through his drug dealings.

I've noted that John was quite charming. He had these piercing blue eyes that seemed to look right through you. He knew just what to say and was intelligent and worldly. He was really good with animals, and I think he used that and what I'll call his animal magnetism to attract women, including me. I met him when I was completely disenchanted with my life and ready to head back to Ohio with my son. Then along came John; life with him and Rachel would be my savior.

I just wanted to please him so he would pay attention to me. Whenever my behavior caused an outburst, I would just change it. Years later, I realized I was being slowly but surely brainwashed. I was never any good at standing up for myself. I was easily manipulated so that I went along willingly.

I've come to see that my tendency for that stemmed from how things were after my father died. It was such a critical time. I had so many questions about so many things, especially about our religion, but I was afraid to ask. Mom had so much on her plate, I couldn't ask her – I didn't want to be another problem for her. So, I just faded into the background and lived vicariously through friends and my imagination.

I didn't feel I had much worth, so I tried to fit in with everyone. With my preppy friends, I became preppy. With my hoodlum friends, I talked and acted like them. With my family, I was who they wanted me to be. Each persona was completely sincere, but still a form of play-acting. I guess that's why I ended up searching for a savior, something I could believe in, and an identity – to find self-value. I believed this life with John and

Rachel was the answer and I was determined to stick with it, whatever it took.

Rachel was the oldest girl in an American Indian family of four boys and two girls. At nine or ten years old, she was forced to attend a government boarding school in Chicago hundreds of miles from her family – part of a program to help Native Americans assimilate into the world of white people. Her father began molesting her when she was about eleven. Her mom was probably aware of the abuse but did nothing about it. Rachel contracted venereal disease, which left her unable to have children. She also started drinking and doing drugs at an early age.

Her father and mother were from different Northern California tribes, but lived on the same reservation. It was a very troubled place to grow up. Crime, incest, drug and alcohol abuse were the norm, as were rampant prejudice and murder among the tribes and between the Caucasians and the Indians. It is like that even today.

John rescued her from all that when she was 18. He was 19 and they became inseparable. I guess the odd, nomadic life they had together was better than anything she had ever known. And, instead of trying to make her white, he embraced her native culture.

At some point during the first few weeks of our relationship, I met Rachel's brothers. Except for one brother, Les, they didn't like John. When they found out about me they came to see what was going on. I guess I met their approval because they didn't do anything to harm me. I was too naïve to be scared, but I should have been. They were really big guys, and I came to know they could be dangerous to anyone they thought was a threat to them or their family.

Rachel's sister came around, too. Like Rachel and her brothers, she was tough. Being raised on the reservation made people tough; everyone, old or young, man or woman, knew how to fight and to win. I witnessed some brutal fights. Gender didn't matter; they all fought with one another and they would use anything at hand for a weapon – bats, boards, bricks, you name it.

I found out later that John had once asked Rachel's sister to become his wife, too. I never credited her with having much sense, but apparently, she had more than I. John also tried to give me to one of his friends. I don't know if Rachel had anything to do with it or not; she was never slow to remind me I wasn't the only woman he tried to recruit into the family. He and Rachel had practically raised each other; they had been together for six years and had been through a lot before I came along. That left me feeling I had no rights as a wife.

She was already showing signs of jealousy, and as I was to realize later, she never forgot a wrong and always got her revenge. I couldn't see that I was just a commodity to John, while I didn't want anyone but him. I was so blind, so enchanted with it all. Because Rachel never spoke up, I just assumed things between us were all right. Time taught me that I was very wrong about that. She did her best to get back at me over the years, pretending friendship just to betray me. The truth was, we were both so selfish that we didn't stop to think about the other's feeling. All we cared about was ourselves.

Nevertheless, the reality of their tormented and abusive early years left me very grateful for my good childhood. I thought I was doing something positive by showing them that they could be part of a good family. In response, they only ridiculed me for being brought up in a fantasy world. Theirs was the real world; I was weak and stupid and my family had no clue what the world was really like.

They were both drug and alcohol dependent. Many years later, they gave up alcohol, but the drugs never stopped. Not with them and not with me. They started out with pot and speed, but it got to the point there wasn't a substance they didn't abuse, including meth, crack-cocaine, opium and shooting speedballs, a combination of speed, cocaine and heroin or morphine.

34

I just was a little bit more discriminating, sticking mostly to pot and psychedelics. I also tried heroin once, cocaine and crack a few times, and smoked opium some. As bad as it all was, the worst I witnessed was John, Rachel and others sniffing glue. I tried it once, and never again – it was horrible!

My memories of seeing people sitting on the floor with a glue-filled paper bag held up to their face still haunt me. Their eyes would glaze over and they could only keel over, with glue dripping off their noses. John and Rachel also shot up speed. That stuff scared me so badly I never tried it. I watched as they tied off and put the needles in their arms, then top it off with Jack Daniels and pot to take the edge off.

The details escape me now, but the three of us and the kids once drove to Nogales, Mexico, to get drugs. Word on the street was you could get almost anything over the counter. We stayed in some fleabag motel and went to pharmacies, buying anything we thought might get us high. Of course, to get back across the border we had to hide the drugs. Rachel and I really came in handy for that; we put the vials of drugs inside us and drove through the checkpoint. We weren't searched. But were we ever stupid!

They were always very secretive about our life. This was partly because they both had warrants out on them, and also because, if I wanted to be with them, I had to leave everything behind. They didn't want anyone to know who or where they were. I had to show complete loyalty.

I think they saw a treasure trove in me because they could control me, I was clean, had no criminal record and looked innocent enough to always play the front man when there was a problem with the police or other authorities and I had a valid driver's license.

Their control and my willingness showed itself early on. I was so excited about my new life with John and Rachel, I called my mother to tell her about it. I blurted out everything about being a co-wife and living off the land and making native jewelry and crafts to earn money. John and Rachel stood right there with me listening to every word and telling me what to say and not say. Naturally, I left out the part about welfare fraud and bounced checks and taking my son without the consent of his father. Who would not see or hear from him for two decades or more.

So what if we were always dancing with danger! I couldn't imagine being a part of a more exciting lifestyle. Besides, there were guns, Indians and horses involved. Maybe as a kid, I watched too much TV about the wild West.

Chapter 5
Nomads

So, we left off with the three of us and Rocky having to get out of town, leaving welfare fraud, bad checks and assault in our wake.

Before we could go too far, we had to find a place to board Tomahawk, John's stallion. We borrowed a horse trailer and took him inland where there was room to pasture him. The owners of the property were the same people he purchased his horse from. While we were fencing off some pasture for Tomahawk, someone came by and asked if John would help load some horses into a trailer. Like so many of our adventures, it didn't go very well.

First, they had to catch the horses. One mare was so freaked out by the trailer and being tied up that she reared and bucked and nearly impaled herself on a post. After a while, they gave her a horse tranquilizer to calm her down. They finally got a halter on her, then led her to the trailer with one person in front and three behind her, with a rope across her hind end to push her into the trailer.

The tranquilizer wasn't nearly effective enough. She began rearing again and kept hitting her head

37

on the trailer. She began stomping, bucking and kicking.

She was finally subdued and tied to a post, but soon got her wind back and then knocked herself out by slamming into the post. She soon died from the shock of it all. It was awful. I've never seen anything like it. It's hard to believe none of the people involved were injured or killed.

After getting Tomahawk settled, we returned to the Newport area so John could do some fishing with a friend to earn some money. We stayed on the same property where I was living when I met John. I was pregnant by this time. We kept a very low profile so no one would find out we were back in the area.

We then headed up to Portland to sell some of our handmade leather goods. While there, we picked up a friend who wanted to go with us to Bagby Hot Springs in Mt. Hood National Forest. We hiked up the mountain to the hot springs and camped out there for a day. We continued hiking for another full day, headed up to a secluded trout lake. Rocky was doing pretty well until he fell off the trail and went down about a hundred feet or so. Thank God, he wasn't hurt but it took some doing to get him back up to the trail again.

We got to the campsite at dusk, hungry, tired and cold, with only a few potatoes and some jalapeno peppers. It was June and the mountain was snowcapped. We had no fishing poles or bait, so after setting up a camp, we made fishing poles from branches. We had some line and hooks and made flies with material from a blouse I was wearing. It was too late to fish, so we went to bed as hungry, tired and cold as when we arrived.

The next morning Rachel decided we should all go swimming in the freezing, rushing river, and since you didn't argue with Rachel, we all went "swimming", almost being swept away by the current. In just a few minutes, numbness set in. Then the guys decided to go fishing again. They were successful, and we ate like kings, devouring rainbow trout, chili peppers and potatoes roasted over an open fire. With full stomachs and the sun shining warmly on us, we headed back down the mountain, stopping for a bath in the hot springs.

As we headed south on our way back to Portland, the truck broke down on the freeway on-ramp. We were there for three days before we figured out what was wrong and got it running again, sleeping in the truck and walking to the nearest store or fast food restaurant to buy food. As we got underway, we decided to go visit Rachel's family in Salem. We stored some of our possessions with them, then returned to Newport in anticipation of magic mushroom season.

In Newport, we stayed with a couple and their three children. The oldest was the same age as Rocky. The couple was also good friends with Herk, so he soon showed up. John met him at the door with a threat. He left but came back with the police. John had Rocky and me hide in an attic closet while they searched for us. They didn't find us, but what happened during the search was hilarious.

The couple was into making beer and had stored the capped bottles in spots all over the house while the beer aged; the house that was nice and toasty from the wood stove. The heat activated the yeast in the beer, so the bottles started exploding – throughout the house! I think the police were laughing so hard about this that they forgot all about searching for us.

John wanted me and Rocky to go stay with some friends in a nearby town; they came to pick us up in the dark of night so we could leave undetected. He and Rachel would join us the next day after they borrowed some money, using the truck as collateral so we had no vehicle. Rachel called her brother and he came and drove them to meet us. We returned to Salem to stay with her family.

We convinced one of Rachel's relatives to drive us to California to visit friends and family on the reservation. While there, we decided to go visit Annie Lake, well known for her skill in weaving

Pomo Indian baskets. We were interested in having her teach us. Rachel, Rocky and I camped on her property on the Rancheria in Redwood Valley, while John returned to Oregon to trade and buy supplies, and to continue with magic mushroom season.

Annie let us tag along with her as she gathered willow branches and sedge root by the creek bed. Then we sat on the porch and watched her as she prepared the roots and branches and began to weave. She spoke only her native Pomo tongue, so there was no verbal teaching – we could only sit and watch to learn. What a privilege, especially for me, a non-native. Pomo baskets are world-renowned; they are both water-tight and beautiful. Some have beads or feathers woven into the design. After Annie's death, Rachel was probably one of only a handful of indigenous people who had mastered this art.

I was six months pregnant when John returned from Oregon with his friend, David. They arrived in an older Volkswagen bug they bought for $50. It was a real gem – the brakes were worn to the metal, wheel bearings needed to be replaced, and we usually had to push it and then pop the clutch to get it running. They left us the car and hitchhiked back to Oregon for the rest of mushroom season.

Rachel didn't drive, so I became the driver & mechanic. The nearest town was about 5 miles from Annie's place, so when we needed to go there, it took Rocky, Rachel and me to get the bug going. With the key on, I'd position myself by the open car door and push, while Rachel and Rocky pushed from the rear. When it was rolling good, I and my huge belly would jump into the driver's seat and pop the clutch. Then Rachel and Rocky would jump in and off we'd go.

Sometimes we'd take Annie to the Indian Center in town so she could visit with old friends and have a free lunch of Indian fry bread, fried seaweed and surf fish; of course, we joined in the free lunch whenever we could.

I couldn't rely on the car's brakes, so I stopped by downshifting. There were some close calls as we drove around on the hilly roads. The car would get us up the hills, then I'd put it in neutral and coast down. Not such a safe thing to do, but it sure saved a lot of gas! Anyway, since when had I shown any good sense whatsoever in my life with John and Rachel? I often think of the countless times God must have sent His angels to look after us in all our dances with danger.

John and David finally returned from Oregon. We had become truly afraid that a wheel would fall of the bug, among all its other problems, so we drove it to the nearest junkyard, barely making it to the lot, and hit the chain link fence to get it to stop. The owner traded another old wreck for it; we managed to drive around in that sedan for a while.

Once, while heading up to Oregon in the sedan, we stopped for a break at a motel in Arcata, California. While there, I started having side pains; I was pregnant and not sure if that had anything to do with the pain or not. John thought I just needed to stay put and rest, so he and Rachel left his friend David and Rocky with me and continued on to Oregon. The pain got much worse. So, Rocky in hand, I walked 10 blocks to a free clinic I knew of in town – in excruciating pain the whole time. They didn't know what to do with me, so sent me to the Mad River hospital emergency room.

The hospital determined I had appendicitis and admitted me. I had no idea who was watching over Rocky and couldn't think straight in all my agony and fear. I finally found out that someone at the clinic was taking care of him. So, I told them where to find David and that he would come and take care of Rocky. Later, they came to the hospital to see me, but the nursing staff wouldn't allow Rocky into my room because he was too young. So, they showed up at the window of my room to visit, which was on the ground floor. We talked and I made sure Rocky was in good hands until I was released from the hospital.

I was alone, very afraid, and had to decide whether or not to let the doctor operate, knowing if I didn't agree to that, the appendix might burst. Either way, I was frantic about whether the baby would be okay. I called my mother collect and told her the situation. She was afraid for me and thought the only thing to do was pray and go ahead with the operation.

I did just that. After the operation, I was unable to even roll over in bed. The slightest movement shot unbearable pain over my right side and belly. After about three days, John and Rachel returned from Oregon and came to check on me. Deciding I was in good hands, they took Rocky and David and headed back to Oregon with plans to return in a week. I figured I would be in the hospital until they came back, but then the doctor decided to release me after only two days.

I could barely walk with the crutches they gave me and had to hold my stomach up to relieve the pressure on the stitches. This is when I found out that my appendix was not in danger of bursting after all. Bed rest would have been all I needed. I think the doctors wanted to get me out of the hospital as soon as possible so I wouldn't make any complaints.

I had nowhere to go, had no money and didn't know anyone. Once again, God must have been watching out for me because two women from the free clinic came to my rescue. They picked me up at the hospital, made sure I had prescriptions and vitamins, then took me home to care for me. Somehow, I got word to John where to find me, and put in a call to my mother to let her know I was okay. John, Rachel and Rocky showed up in a few days, and as nuts as it was, we all piled in the old wreck of a car and headed back to Oregon.

Of course, I needed more recovery time. It worked out that I could stay with the couple who owned the property where I lived when I met John. John, Rachel and Rocky stayed in the cabin. The husband was a commercial fisherman and John went fishing with him to make some money.

I was put-up in a bedroom close to the bathroom. Yeah indoor plumbing! The couple fed and nursed me and even removed my stitches. John and Rachel were very unhappy about that, as they didn't want anyone to touch me without their permission. I was still too stupid to see the problem with that. When I was finally able to travel and had enough money, we got the red truck out of pawn, loaded it up and headed southwest for the winter. John's friend, David, joined us.

The promise of the nomad life lay ahead, our dream was about to unfold. I was excited and full of anticipation.

Chapter 6
Lavina, Tommy and Trouble Ahead

We traveled through California and Arizona to
Phoenix, ending up near Tempe, camping out in
the Superstition Mountains and then the Saguaro
National Monument park in Tucson. It was
beautiful. Big Red, our International Harvester,
had 4-wheel drive so we were able to go into some
of the most remote places. I also learned quickly
how to cook over an open fire. Heavenly!

At Thanksgiving, we went into Tempe and had
dinner at the Salvation Army; they also gave us
groceries and a food voucher. We bought some
more groceries, headed back to camp, and cooked
another turkey and all the trimmings over the
open fire. It was like manna from heaven - what a
feast!

We pulled our mattresses out of the truck and
slept under the stars. Finally, it seemed as if we
were beginning to live the life we planned.

Originally, I had planned to give birth out in the
desert but became somewhat unsure of this idea
as the time for me to give birth approached, so we
rented a little cement block house in the barrio
section of Tucson. It was one room with a
bathroom and an efficiency kitchen. All five of us

packed into this small space and slept on foam mattresses on the cement floor.

At nine months pregnant, I was the one who lugged our laundry to the on-site laundromat; no one offered to help. I guess I could have asked, but it seemed so self-evident. I also waddled my way through most of the cleaning and cooking. John, Rachel and David were too busy selling and trading beadwork and leather crafts, bartering, and looking for drugs to pay much attention to me. Happily, it was January so the nights were cool and the days were pleasantly warm.

I went into labor and Lavina was born before dawn on January 28, 1975. No midwife this time! Just John, Rachel and my son were there for the birth. David slept through it or at least he pretended to thankfully. I coached Rachel and John to do what needed to be done. Truly, God blessed us with Lavina. She had plenty of dark hair and was beautifully formed. I was so thankful that all my fears during the appendectomy episode were only that – fears; it had no effect on her at all. God watches over us fools.

A few weeks after Lavina was born, we decided it was time to get on the road again and explore the southwest. We planned to head north to Flagstaff then east to Gallup and Albuquerque. This was the night we were trapped in the snowstorm, freezing almost to death, until the stranger, the good

Samaritan, showed up and saved our lives. As usual, I can barely breathe as I think of that terrifying night and how Tommy Lee came to our rescue out of nowhere.

Tommy took us to his home, The China Springs Trading Post, located on legendary Route 66 at the edge of the Navajo reservation about 10 miles west of Gallup. The front of the building housed a silver shop on one side and a storage area on the other. We stayed in the middle area, which was once the store. Tommy, a full-blooded Navajo, lived at the back of the building with his Navajo wife, Irene, and their 5 children.

Tommy's living area had three bedrooms, a kitchen, a front room, and a non-functioning bathroom. The only heat was provided by coal burning stoves. We were warm and comfortable enough. John and Tommy became fast friends, and I don't think he ever respected anyone more than he did Tommy.

We all used an outhouse located about 50 feet from the building. If it was a cold or stormy night we utilized a 5-gallon bucket which we dumped the next day. Old newspapers served as our toilet paper. And this was one of the better living accommodations on the reservation. Irene's family owned the land which ran from the highway north for a few miles and west for a few miles They were sheepherders the same as their ancestors had been before them.

Tommy had been a wino for many years, well into his forties. He drifted around, hopping trains. He was in San Francisco staying in a flophouse. One night, he drank himself to sleep, as usual, with his bottle nearby so he could take a swig whenever he wanted. In his dreams that night, he had a vision of Jesus calling him out of the life he was leading. The vision was so strong that when he awoke, he gave his life to Jesus and never had another drink and no delirium tremens. He returned to his reservation and became a preacher. He was in his fifties when we met him.

China Springs was more than just a name; the spring flowed from an outcropping of rocks in a little valley. The sheep drank water from a nearby pool. We dipped water with a bucket through a window cut into the rock. In the winter, we had to use a steel pipe to smash through the half-foot of ice that formed over the wellspring.

In the heat of summer, the water was cool and refreshing. We would climb right inside the wellspring window to sit and cool off with the kids. Baths were few and far between, especially in the winter. When we got desperate, we would go to the spring and just pour water over each other, soap up, and rinse off. Invigorating, for sure! The downside was that the valley smelled of sheep dung. No matter – living off the grid and off the land was a dream come true.

Someone would have to keep a lookout for the sheepherders, especially if we were bathing. If they found us there, we'd be run off because we were white and didn't belong there. They were even suspicious of Rachel because she wasn't Navajo and was with the Anglos.

There we were, "hippies" living in the midst of Navajo Nation, the largest population of Native Americans in North America. People on the reservation heard about us and many would come to Tommy's to check us out. Some without good intentions but Tommy watched out for us.

These were people who still lived the way their ancestors had – in thatched-roof hogans on the high desert with no running water or electricity. They planted corn, beans and squash, herded sheep in the spring and summer, and made beautiful jewelry, pottery and the woven rugs all of which were sought after by collectors. The traders often preyed on them, buying their crafts and making a 200% or more profit.

We didn't have much to read so we often listened to Navajo radio, which was broadcast in the Navajo language, one of the hardest to learn. But we listened anyway hoping to learn a little of the language. They also played country western music which we found amusing. The big radio treat was Mystery Theatre on Friday nights because it was broadcast in English. We weren't smoking pot or using drugs or drinking alcohol because Tommy would not allow it, so the radio was our "drug" while we lived there.

Cabin fever typically set in during the winter so we would have to get out and about to keep from going nuts. We'd usually head for Gallup, the "wino capital of the world", to look through pawn shops or go out to eat at a local diner. We couldn't buy any pot; both because we stood out as hippies living in cowboy territory and because there was just none available. If there was, John would have sniffed it out! Half pints of cheap Thunderbird wine were the drug of choice in the area. We had an occasional beer when we were doing the town.

We needed money, so we decided to apply for food stamps and welfare. This meant I had to get a birth certificate for Lavina. With this I had the bright idea that we should say Rachel was her mother. That way, we would get more money and food stamps than I would have gotten as one mother with two children. We never said anything about John being around or that he was the father. I was becoming a truly effective conniver.

In the spring, we took a trip to Albuquerque to sell and trade some of Tommy's silver and turquoise hatbands and our jewelry. Big Red was still running, but not very well. On our way back to Gallup David and John were drunk and got into an argument, resulting with John putting him out of the truck and on to the highway alone. He had no money and just a few belongings. Even friends were dancing with danger when they hung out with us. No one was immune to John's wrath.

While I wasn't terribly sad to see him go, I felt bad for him and couldn't understand why John treated him so badly. After all, they had been friends longer than I had even been around. It just showed me that I could be next, except for the fact that Lavina was our child. But even that was pretty shaky since her birth certificate was fake.

That same spring, Tommy moved us into a one-room cabin on his property. At the time, we were told and believed a local shaman had put a curse on our family. We attributed the fact to Lavina falling and being burned by the coal stove. She had been around coal stoves since she just a few weeks old and was taught not to touch them. We had no defense against the powers of evil which I know exist. I know now that Tommy was praying for our family which protected us from any further harm.

We built a bed platform, found a sofa for the kids to sleep on, and used a Coleman stove to cook meals. We were about 100 yards downhill from the spring, so had to take 5-gallon jugs up the hill, fill them and then drag them back down the hill. For bathing, we heated water over the coal stove.

We continued to make jewelry and crafts and became quite good at making rings and bracelets from the silver and cabochons of abalone shell we brought from California. Our goal was to make 25 rings every other week. A local trader would buy all we had for $8-$10 each and resell them for $25-$40. We did this for quite a while but never seemed to save much money. We gave Tommy money and spent the rest on beer, food, coal and gas – and trying to keep Big Red running.

Winter came again, which made getting water and supplies even harder, except when the hill was snowy. Then, we could tie the jugs together and slide them down the hill. The following summer, we became friends with a white woman and her daughter who lived in town. She knew where to get pot in spite of its scarcity, so we spent a lot of time with her. John was probably sleeping with her, of course. I think he actually believed he was God's gift to women, not to mention he'd do about anything for some pot.

Late that summer we decided to leave and go back to Oregon. Rachel wanted to spend some time with her family; we also wanted to get our hands on some pot and magic mushrooms. Our Scout was out of commission so we needed a vehicle to get us there.

We had a Dodge sedan for a while that a car dealer let us "borrow" until we acquired a lime green VW bus by barter. We packed up our jewelry, including a beautiful squash blossom necklace to sell for Tommy, and belongings, gathered up the kids and headed for Las Vegas. We left with very little cash and a stolen credit card we had bought from some drunken Indian.

Chapter 7
Downhill All the Way

We made it as far as Chambers, Arizona just 49 miles from Gallup, a little town in the desert where we stopped for gas. I tried to use the credit card to pay for it. No deal. I must have looked guilty and scared because I was guilty and scared. I just knew this wasn't going to go well but, had very little choice. I was arrested and hauled off to jail while my kids watched. I was still nursing Lavina. They fingerprinted me, searched me and put me in a cell until I could see the judge the next day.

John and Rachel followed me to the jail to find out what was going on. They camped out in the parking lot overnight with the kids while I slept in the cell. I was alone, which was a blessing, and prayed pretty hard for my kids' safety and for me to get out of the predicament I'd gotten myself into. I cried out to God and He answered.

I saw the sheriff/judge in his office the following morning. I noticed that he had numerous shelves and glass cases filled with beautiful Indian jewelry and other artifacts, along with a lot of guns and knives. I was intimidated by his demeanor and probably shaking in my sandals because he hinted that sexual favors might be a possibility for getting out of the situation. He verbally gave me the choice of a large fine or jail time. There was the answer to one part of my prayer!

I didn't have the cash, of course, so I asked him if he would trade jewelry for the fine. He wanted to see what I had before he agreed. I was escorted to the van and retrieved our jewelry case and was also able to talk to John and see that my kids were alright. The rest of the answer to my prayers.

Back alone with the judge, I opened our case and discovered we'd inadvertently left Tommy's Squash Blossom necklace in it. Turned out, that's exactly the piece the judge wanted for my fine. I desperately tried to talk him out of it by telling him it didn't belong to me, but he knew he had me so he wouldn't relent. I had no choice but to give it to him.

I was released only to have to face John with the news of the necklace. His reaction was not what I expected – he just said we'd have to pay back Tommy when we could. I think he took the news so well after all we'd been through in the past 24 hours and because he had been saddled with the kids all that time. Perhaps he had a tinge of guilt, who knows? It could have been a lot worse, after all we were dealing with the still somewhat wild west there in the middle of nowhere.

As surprised as I was with John's reaction, I remember thinking that sure was one expensive tank of gas.

We continued our drive, heading north through the Arizona mountains, stopping in Flagstaff to try and sell or trade for our wares. Then on to Las Vegas to a shop Tommy knew that would buy our jewelry. Sure enough, we sold enough to get dinner and a motel room for the night. We spent the next day going door to door to shops and pawnshops selling our crafts and jewelry. Someone suggested we should go to one of the nightclubs near the motel and set up a table to display and sell the jewelry.

John sent Rachel and me to do just that. He knew people would be wary of his looks, his long, braided hair and steely blue eyes. Rachel and I were far less threatening. We went into the club that evening, dressed as nicely as we could, and with the bartender's permission, set up the jewelry. We sat, waited and watched as people arrived and the music began to play. After about an hour, we realized we were in a gay bar. We didn't sell much jewelry, but we got an eyeful!

We soon had enough of Las Vegas. We took the kids to a free breakfast buffet and while waiting in line, Rachel put a few coins in a slot machine and won more money than we had made the whole time we were there. Go figure. We wanted to keep that money, so we gassed up and headed out of town without delay. While heading north through the mountains in California we started to have engine trouble. Little did we know that Volkswagens had oil-cooled engines and we had never checked or put any oil in it since we acquired it. We made it to a used car dealer and traded for an American-made sedan then loaded up our belongings and the kids and headed out again. We arrived in Salem, Oregon a few days later. There we stayed for a couple of months.

The day before Christmas, Rachel and her sister and sister-in-law decided to go Indian Christmas shopping – also known as shoplifting. John, Rachel's brother, Rocky, Lavina and I all piled into one car and her sister, sister-in-law and other brother in another car. We hit the department store. The kids and I were there for distraction. I had never been involved with anything like that before. It was amazing how much they got away with! They put layers of clothes on and stuffed things down their pants and under their loose-fitting blouses. I was terrified. I didn't dare try it myself, I am sure I looked guilty as hell.

When we were done at the department store, we went grocery "shopping". We bought a few small things while they proceeded to stuff steaks and roasts and all kinds of items into their pants. We were in the car about to leave when someone was found out. The police were there in no time. We managed to drive off but they pursued us. Yikes! Being chased by the police with sirens blaring, speeding down the main thoroughfare. We made it back to the house and, as soon as the car stopped, everyone was out and running in every direction.

I took the kids to the bathroom, locked the door, started running a bath, got them undressed and into the tub. The police broke down the front door and proceeded to trash everything in sight. They threw down the Christmas tree and stomped all the presents, then they went searching for people. They had one of Rachel's brothers in handcuffs and John in a chokehold with a nightstick. Rachel was beating on the cop to make him let go of John before he killed him.

They made their way to the bathroom and broke in the door to find us. They took a look around and just left.

I was praying a lot by then, and as I have found to be true through the years, God answers prayer even if we don't begin to deserve it. He doesn't sit there waiting to whack us for doing wrong, He actually waits for opportunities to be gracious to us. After it was all over, Rachel's two brothers and John were in jail. Her other older brother, who was not involved, had some connections with civil rights lawyers and the American Indian Movement

(AIM) and somehow managed to get everyone released on technicalities the next day.

We didn't stick around Salem much longer. When it seemed safe, we went to Santa Rosa, California, and stayed at Rachel's grandmother's house until spring, making jewelry and leather goods, living off food stamps, commodities and whatever we could glean from the local farm fields. We ate a lot of cauliflower that month – cauliflower soup, baked cauliflower, fried cauliflower, cauliflower casserole, cauliflower you-name-it. John and a friend did some hunting so we ate venison and duck, too. Rachel's grandmother had gone back to live on the reservation because there was a lien on the house.

When spring came the house was sold, so we went to live on Rachel's reservation in Covelo, California. We camped out at Hull's Valley a few miles up in the foothills. Once there, and our camp was set up, John and Rachel decided to go on a drinking binge with her brother and cousins, leaving me and the kids to fend for ourselves. Rachel's older cousin had a cabin nearby, so some mornings we went there to eat pancakes. I helped tend a little garden, which we watered by hand from a spring about 50 yards away. We weren't very successful; it was summertime, very hot and dry, so water was running low.

There was also a raspberry patch a mile or so from our campsite so the kids and I would go pick raspberries but had to watch for rattlesnakes. I learned to make raspberry pie on a wood fire – an interesting endeavor – but it tasted great. After the kids and I had been on our own for a few days, we were running out of food and in dire need of a bath and clean clothes.

I decided to hike down the mountain and go into town for showers and supplies. With Lavina in a backpack and Rocky in tow, we started down the dirt road. We had walked a couple of miles when a farmer came by in his truck and gave us a ride. I took the kids to a local hotel for showers and did some laundry and food shopping. It was a wonder that I had any money.

I was challenged by the prospect of getting the three of us and the supplies back up the hill to camp, but all I could do was give it my best. As we headed up, John, Rachel and a carload of drunken Indians came by and drove us to the campsite. Then they took off again. I didn't wonder much that someone was watching over us. As usual, though, I soon forgot it and went on with life.

When they were done with their partying, John and Rachel returned with some old friends from Santa Rosa. We hiked down to a secluded spot on the Eel River and went skinny-dipping. As if it didn't matter to me that they left us high and dry, as if there wasn't a problem in the world. I was angry and resentful but didn't dare say a word. Later on, we got a ride to Santa Rosa and went to Robert's house, an old friend of John's. He let us stay for a while and in exchange, John taught him silversmithing.

We finally had some money from selling some of our crafts and some drug deals. Robert let me and Rachel borrow his car so we could go get the truck we had to leave in Oregon out of pawn. Because of the warrants out for his arrest, John didn't have a driver's license, and neither did Rachel. So, for years I did most of the driving as well as acted as the front man since I looked so sweet and innocent. It took years for this to become burdensome for me. For the driving and everything else I did, I began to feel used and left to do all the dirty work while they just waited in the background or did whatever they wanted.

So, I did most of the driving up to Oregon. In order to have all the money we needed to get the truck and gas for the return trip, we had to sell and pawn some things. We even went back to Salem to get the belongings we had to leave behind. The truck was hard to drive; it still needed some work on the steering and the brakes were bad. Rachel followed me in Robert's car.

Trying to deal with the steering, I was all over the road like a drunk – in a half-ton truck! The brakes were so unreliable I had to downshift or pull the emergency brake to get it to slow down or stop. And of course, most of the trip was downhill. It was gut-wrenching, but we made it back in one piece. Always dancing with danger.

There is a verse in the Bible that says: For He causes His sun to rise on the evil and the good and sends rain on the righteous and the unrighteous. (Matthew 5:45 NASB). So true. Whether I realized it or not, He took care of me and of us in the midst of our worst foolishness, even though almost anyone would have correctly pegged us as unworthy.

I also see now that mostly downhill trip from Oregon turned out to be a preview of what lay ahead.

Chapter 8
The Dream Takes a Detour

While in Santa Rosa, we met up with another of John's old drug friends, Manuel. So, for the first time, I began to mess around with hard drugs – speed and heroin. I had already witnessed glue-sniffing; it was so horrible that I wanted no part of it. I passed over other opportunities for hard drugs because I was nursing. But there was nothing holding me back this time.

John and Rachel used speed intravenously before I met them, so they were quite adept at it. They indulged for a while and one night in a motel room I got talked into trying a little heroin. I was so scared of it that my body must have rejected it because I didn't feel a thing. Plus, they weren't too keen on sharing their fix so they didn't give me much of a dose.

While they stayed up all night in the motel bathroom doing speedballs, the kids and I slept in the bed. I now thank God for saving me from that one – among so many other dangers. Of course, I didn't see it that way at the time and used my share of cocaine and crack.

We were staying in the motel because Robert's girlfriend wanted us out of their place. We had been hearing so much about Sausalito, a community where everyone lived on boats in the San Francisco bay, we wanted to experience it. It was also a fresh opportunity to sell and trade our jewelry and crafts. The drugs had such a hold on John and Rachel, we literally had to wrench ourselves away from Santa Rosa, but we did it.

We were enjoying the whole Sausalito experience when John basically disappeared for several days, supposedly in the midst of some drug deal. We got worried and started searching, ultimately hearing that he was out on a boat in the bay. Somehow, we got him back on land; he was high and drunk and had no idea where he was or what he was doing. We scooped him up, put him in the truck and drove off. Not our best Sausalito experience!

We soon drained all our resources doing all the drugs we could get our hands on. Somehow, we managed to trade the truck for another International van, a white one this time, and decided to head back to Tucson and the barrio where Lavina was born.

We rented a very small, very old one-bedroom trailer infested with rats – until we were kicked out for not paying the rent. Any money we got from working, pawning or selling things went for drugs, drugs and more drugs. They really had their claws in us. I mostly stuck to pot and psychedelics, but I was always right in the thick of the drug use and fully contributing to it.

I got a job in the catering department of a large hotel in Tucson, serving at parties and entertainment events. Most of what I earned went to drugs. Often, John would come there and take whatever tips I'd received so he could make a drug deal somewhere. On the upside, I got to see B.B. King, the Dave Brubeck Band and other popular performers up close and for free. I was pregnant again and worked there until I was about five months along.

After we were kicked out of the trailer, we moved into a little stucco house in the barrio. We got kicked out of that after a month by one irate landlord because John decided to paint the bathroom with red and black enamel. If it wasn't one thing, it was twelve others!

Then we camped out in the desert for a little while until John and Rachel joined a craft co-op and started making jewelry again. We always had our equipment with us, no matter where we went. We made a little money on the crafts and John made a whole lot more on drug deals, so we were able to rent a three-bedroom house on Stone Street, of all things. The perfect street name for us! It was one of the best places we ever lived, with a nice yard. I created a little garden and even John joined in tending it.

The van stopped running soon after we moved to Stone Street and it sat in the driveway from then on. We got around on foot, by bus, bicycle or by hitchhiking. We didn't have much money left after paying for rent and drugs. Even the few food stamps I received were usually traded for cash or drugs. So, we ate out of grocery store and food suppliers' dumpsters. We ate fairly well. Lots of fruits and veggies. One time we found a crate of eggs thrown out because a few in every carton were cracked and broken. We ate a lot of eggs for a while!

One day Lavina became very ill with a high fever and began to convulse. We decided to take her to the emergency room. After dunking her in icy water several times to get her temperature to drop, the doctor had us hold her down while they did a spinal tap. It was awful; she was only three! We were all so traumatized by the experience that we took her home even though the doctor wanted to keep her there.

I kept bathing her in tepid water as my mother taught me, until her fever went down. Then I began a regimen of crushed vitamin C tablets mixed with honey washed down with goldenseal herb tea with honey. I gave it to her every three hours for three days. Best I could tell, she was almost in a coma.

We were never sure what caused her to become so ill. John put forward the theory that she might have eaten some poisonous plant from the yard. I wonder now if she got into some of the drugs. Maybe it was germs from the dumpster food. Who knows. What I do know for sure is that, once again, God was watching over us; Lavina recovered with no ill effects.

Around this same time, Rocky ran away from home. He was about six years old. He didn't have any toys, so he had been playing with a stick and accidentally hurt Lavina. Rachel got angry and told him to go away. He thought she meant forever. I searched all over and finally called the police. They found him a few blocks away playing with some kids. When they asked him who he was, he lied because he had been taught not to trust the police. It turned out he was trying to adopt a new family. Who could blame him? I was so wrapped up in myself, I had no idea what he was going through at the time.

John was obviously the restless type. I was getting hugely pregnant and he and Rachel were having some hellacious fights, usually about drugs. So, poor John wasn't getting the attention he wanted. He started spending a lot of time at the park buying and selling drugs. He met a young homeless woman; I'll call her Allison. By pretending to want to become a Buddhist, she often stayed at the local Ashram.

John decided to ask her to stay with us. Foolish person that I was, I thought nothing of it. Rachel was much more suspicious. I woke up early one morning to find John and Allison sleeping on the sofa together. He tried to convince me that it was okay and not tell Rachel. He wanted us to agree to Allison becoming his wife, also. I was just confused and hurt, but conniving Rachel played it cool until she could get her revenge.

One day, Rachel and I were sitting on the front steps waiting for Allison to show up from her daily bike ride. When she returned and opened the gate to come in, Rachel hit her with a hurled brick. Allison ran off. John went to the park to find her, but Rachel followed him and they got into a huge argument. That was the last we saw of Allison; but I think John kept seeing her on the sly. I often wondered why Rachel didn't run me off, too.

In his great wisdom, John decided to trade a room in the house for drugs, which led to a dark and terrible time in our lives. Through his drug deals, he had gotten to know a biker and his nurse girlfriend. She was stealing Demerol and morphine in the cancer ward where she worked. John,

Rachel and that couple were usually so strung out it was almost unbearable to be around them.

That ugly episode came to an abrupt end when the nurse was caught, fired, and arrested. The biker took off, never to be seen again. Good riddance! I was seven months pregnant, trying to keep the kids protected from what was going on around them and trying to keep things normal. After all, I was very pregnant, riding a bicycle everywhere, scrounging our food from the dumpsters, and living among drug dealers and drug busts. Yep, we were living the dream and things were perfectly normal.

When the dust cleared from that insanity, John and Rachel kicked from hard drugs and decided we needed to rent out our front bedroom again, but this time to help pay the rent. It was a nice room, light and airy, with French doors leading to the front yard. He invited his friend Lyman to rent it. Lyman turned out to be a pretty decent guy. He was younger, but he worked, paid his rent and was no trouble whatsoever. He stayed for six weeks, until he met a girl and got married.

I went into labor in the early morning hours of St. Patrick's Day in 1978. Lyman and his wife were visiting at the house. I thought I was an expert at this home birth thing and planned it carefully. I prepared a birthing kit and practiced my breathing.

John decided he had plenty of time to go to work at the co-op for a while and then get home in time for the birth. I suspected he had a date with Allison because we called him at work from a nearby pay phone and he was never there. Rachel acted as midwife; Lyman and his wife helped.

When the time for the delivery came, an arm came out first, so Rachel had to tuck it back in and move the baby so the head would come first. As the head emerged, Rachel saw that the umbilical cord was wrapped around the baby's neck, so she slipped it off – just in time, I guess. I had to wonder how riding around on a bicycle when I was nine months pregnant might have contributed to the complications.

John made it home sometime later, and only somewhat tipsy. He named our baby girl Snow. We didn't have a scale, but soon weighed her on a grocery store scale when no one was looking. I guessed her birth weight to be less than seven pounds, the smallest baby I had given birth to. She was healthy, strong and happy, though.

When Snow was about one month old, the Tucson weather was heating up and our finances were in poor shape. We had no car and were being evicted once again. Welfare and food stamps don't go very far when you use them for drugs instead of rent. There was also conflict at the crafts co-op where

John and Rachel worked. They were spending more than they were making, not honoring the rules, and my guess is they probably stole something, too.

So, I called my mother in Cleveland and asked if we could come stay with her until we could get on our feet again. I was convinced that we would be accepted as we were and that I was always welcome to come back. She had never seen Snow or Lavina, and Rocky was only nine months old when she last saw him. She allowed me to come and bring my family. John and Rachel were not so sure about all this, but I convinced them it would be fine.

To this day, I still can't imagine why I didn't have a clue what a really bad idea this was.

Chapter 9
What Was I Thinking?

I just wanted to see my mother, brothers and sisters. I wanted them to see that I was doing fine and had beautiful children and a good family. I needed a break.

To get us to Ohio, I went on a mission to find a drive-away car that needed to be delivered to the Cleveland area. There was a sedan to deliver to Erie, Pennsylvania. It had a cello in the trunk which had to be delivered along with the car. We had about seven days to get it there and, of course, I was expected to do all the driving.

As I was signing the paperwork, my breasts became engorged with milk and started leaking through my top. Very embarrassing! I had to go back home on the bus because I was to pick up the car the next day. I tried my best to hide the stains by walking with a bag in front of me. Always something.

We loaded up the van with the things we couldn't take with us and had it towed to a storage yard. Then with the six of us and the rest of our belongings packed tightly into the car, we headed east. I did most of the driving, especially through the southern states, for fear of being pulled over. Often, I drove while nursing Snow. It was hot. We were crowded. Snow cried a lot, while the other two kids were as good as could be expected spending hours every day in a hot car.

During a break at a Texas truck stop, John and I – well, mostly me – tried to hustle up some gas and food money. Rachel sat in the car with the kids and decided to turn on the radio. She tried to turn the key in the ignition, but it wouldn't turn. So, she put some force into it and the key broke off in the ignition. Turned out she was using the wrong key! As best I can recall, we pushed the car to a shady spot while I called my mother to ask if we could use her AAA membership to have a locksmith come to our rescue.

She agreed and the locksmith came and put in a new ignition. I watched how he did it for future reference. It came in handy more than once. About three days later we arrived in Cleveland, with just enough time to get the sedan to its owner 90 miles away in Erie. After some quick introductions and food, John drove the sedan while I and my sister followed in my mother's car. I probably prayed a lot that the car delivery would take place with no problems, and God graciously answered me. Both the sedan and the cello were delivered on time and in good shape.

My mother was also gracious, as usual. There we were – three small children, two wives along with all our belongings – staying in the basement of her three-bedroom suburban bungalow. My baby sister

Chris was living there, too, soon to be married to her fiancé Dave. Mom also let us use her car to shop and go to flea markets to sell junk and our jewelry, beadwork and leatherwork.

I was receiving food stamps and welfare. We didn't pay rent but bought food for the house. Lavina and Rocky shared the sofa for a bed; Snow, Rachel, John and I slept in a double bed with the baby. This was our usual arrangement. We believed in a family bed, Snow in the middle. Babies slept with us until they were about two years old and weaned. We were not bisexual. Rachel and I gave one another privacy with our husband for intimate times, so nothing kinky was ever part of the picture. As if having two wives was normal.

I found myself feeling quite shy and embarrassed showing any public affection toward John and tried to stay in the background as much as possible. Even in private, unless we were alone together, I kept my distance so as not to make Rachel jealous. Still, I found that the longer we were together, jealousy reared its head more and more each year. I often complained about not being able to go places with John and do things with him as his wife. Eventually, I wore down and learned not to expect the thing I craved most – emotional intimacy with my husband.

Basically, we were mooching off my mom and disrespecting her home. My future brother-in-law was not happy we were there. One evening about three days before he and my sister were to be married, he got into an argument with John about smoking pot in the house. Rachel went after him with a baseball bat. It was easy to see that it was time for us to move on.

By this time, we had acquired a school bus from an Islamic school and were fixing it up to be our mobile home. It was parked in a church lot near the house. John had us go get the bus, pack it up and get ready to leave. My sister's wedding was coming up and I really wanted to be there, so I talked John into letting me go and take the kids while he and Rachel stayed clear of Dave.

I was so happy to be at the wedding and was having a great time seeing all my relatives, yet I suddenly felt this pull that I needed to leave. I somehow convinced myself that my family was just naïve and that I couldn't ever live that straight life again. What was I thinking coming here?

Later, after John and Rachel were out of the house, I went back to talk to my Mom about the argument between Dave and John. I ended up making her cry because I said things to her that I will always regret. I went on the offensive by taking John's side and refusing to see that I was to blame in any way. After apologizing and crying with her, I said goodbye and told her I would call. Oh, what I put my poor mother through over the years. Now, I have experienced a taste of the heartache she went through as I watch my children make some of the mistakes that I made. Even now I really don't know what I was thinking.

I don't know what I was thinking when I talked John and Rachel into going to Cleveland in the first place. I don't know what I was thinking in subjecting my family to my lifestyle. Somehow, I had convinced myself that I had a great life. It certainly was not boring! I wasn't thinking of our kids and what effect all this was having on them, I thought they were fine, and even better off than most kids – traveling around, seeing the world.

I was always stoned and it was easier to do what I was told to do rather than argue or disagree. I didn't want to ruin my buzz. Whatever I said always seemed to come out wrong and made things worse. I was very good at making stupid choices and thinking myself wise. I remember saying a little silent prayer about whatever snafu we were facing at the time. Actually, I had no idea what I was doing and had no awareness that God was actually answering the prayers I said in my head. But He was.

I was afraid to disappoint John and afraid of what Rachel might say if I slipped up on anything. I was afraid to speak up about the kids. I was afraid I'd miss out on all the good times that I was sure were ahead after we got through whatever crisis we were dealing with. So self-centered. Avoiding any conflict by any means, at any cost. Lying to save myself from a tongue-lashing. I learned it was better to bite my tongue rather than experience the wrath of both Rachel and John. I never realized until a few years ago how messed up I was.

There we were a Cleveland winter almost upon us, all of us riding around in this yellow school bus with "Mohammed University" printed on the side, with no place to park it. We hadn't driven around too long before an argument broke out between John, Rachel and me. The details have faded, but I remember it had something to do with my being against them and disloyal to the family. That's where I usually ended up–left holding the bag.

They insisted I take my kids and get out and call my mom to come get us. I found myself with the baby and Rocky (they kept Lavina with them) all alone in a parking lot looking for a phone. I was crying and had no idea what to do. I couldn't bring myself to call my mom after all I'd done and said. I was so ashamed. I went back to the bus and pleaded with them not to leave us. After a lot of crying and begging they let me back in.

In retrospect, I think this was probably the first of many opportunities God provided for me to get out of the crazy life I was living. Instead, I stubbornly held on to my dream of traveling around in our bus, having our own business, living off the land, and eventually settling into a home built with our own hands. The kids needed their father and I needed a husband, not to mention they were going to take my daughter from me.

Because he was our leader and master, I believed John made the decision that night to keep me in the family. Now I know it wasn't John making the decisions, it was Rachel. Sometimes I told myself that I was happy and this is what I wanted. I gave no thought to whether living this way was best for my children; it was all about me. I was a very foolish woman.

I remember thinking that I was doing all this for our family. I'll do anything for him. I will lie for him. Beg if I have to. Anything he says, I'll do; it's for us all. The children needed to eat. My innocent face was needed to put forward whenever trouble came along. I was the one who talked to the cops whenever we were stopped.

We had perfected the art of switching drivers while the bus was moving. John wouldn't let me drive otherwise. I was perfectly capable, but really didn't want to because he would criticize every move I made, to the point I could not function. In

79

the face of that, I preferred my place in the back of the bus anytime.

That's what I was thinking.

With winter coming, we headed south. We stopped for several days in North Carolina, cleaning rooms at a motel and stopping at flea markets to sell our goods. It was near Thanksgiving and our goal was Key West by Christmas.

We made it.

Chapter 10
What Kind of Life This Was

Once we got to Key West, we began exploring the island. After asking around, we found a band of vagabonds like ourselves in vans, motor homes, and converted school buses camping out on various beaches, a practice which was later banned by authorities. We met people who lived on their boats and came ashore to shop or to sell drugs, riding up and down the beach on their bicycles. For me, this was an extraordinary way to live. Of course, we were always high so I probably believed all kinds of things were extraordinary that really weren't.

John never ran out of pot, no matter what. It came before food. "No hope without dope," he always said. I had a continual buzz going on inside my head; I felt fuzzy all the time. Unfortunately, it only added to my tendency to be docile and compliant. John and Rachel were drinking and, believe me, a drunken Indian and a drunken Irishman is not a pretty sight.

The kids and I would steer clear of them as much as possible. A favorite tactic was to pretend to be sleeping when they got into one of their horrendous fights, throwing things and screaming like banshees. John would often get so mad he would start punching the bus or a tree – whatever was close. Better than one of us, I guess! He hurt his hand many times. Rachel was an even worse drunk, belligerent and mean, wanting to fight and hurt someone, anyone.

Then there were the drugs: Quaaludes, downers, others. Rachel had to do whatever John was doing and I mean tit for tat. Drink for drink, pill for pill, line for line, injection for injection. She was his female counterpart and his soul mate; at least that is what I came to believe. I often felt I was just a bystander, a handmaid, only around to have children and take care of the domestic stuff. I was jealous of all the attention she got and deeply frustrated by how she so often manipulated situations to make me come out on the bottom.

I knew she was whispering evil things about me or Rocky in John's ear to turn him against us. It often worked. We were the brunt of many a falling out. He came near to beating me a couple of times; he got mad at me for looking the wrong way at him or for standing up for my son. Rocky got some pretty bad whippings.

I got pushed around some, but mostly I was verbally abused. I cried a lot, for sure. I still cannot understand why I continued to love this man and want so much to be with him. I began to hate Rachel but tried to hide it. I was extra careful around her, always trying to please her, waiting on her, serving her, cleaning up after her. I wanted

John to see what a good woman I was. He never acknowledged me for any of it, but still I kept on. Perseverance is supposed to be an admirable quality, in the Bible, it's a fruit of the Holy Spirit. But, I was merely being a people-pleaser, so that fruit was rotten through and through!

We were running out of money, food stamps and dope, so John got a job in Geronimo's Jewelry Shop on Duval Street in Key West. He made jewelry and helped run the shop. He got close to Geronimo – who was not really an American Indian and not really a jewelry shop merchant. His real business was smuggling drugs from Mexico. Soon Rachel was also working at Geronimo's shop.

Both John and Rachel were adept at sleight of hand and pilfered a few extra dollars here and there when no one would notice. The kids and I would camp on the beach until they were off work. I drove the bus around Key West to do shopping, laundry and other errands.

There was a film crew in Key West making a movie about a local icon, Capt. Tony. There were open auditions for extras, and they hired Rocky to play the part of Capt. Tony's son. I took him over to the hotel where the auditions were being held. We were running late and I had to change the baby, so he went inside alone. By the time I got in there, he had the part!

They shot the movie for about a month, and Rocky was in quite a few scenes. The cast and crew loved him and treated him like a little prince. They fed him, bought him toys, and gave him a new mask, swim fins and snorkel as a going-away gift. He got paid about $150.

Stuart Whitman played Capt. Tony, Robert Vaughn played the bad guy and the producer's girlfriend was the female lead. A host of locals and wannabe actors completed the cast. The movie title started out as "To Kill Castro" but was changed to "Cuba Crossing". The movie itself went nowhere, but Rocky had a ball taking part in the filming.

After some time, we rented a house on Margaret Street in Key West. We parked the bus on the street, moved in our paltry collection of foam mattresses, jewelry-making equipment, dive gear, clothes, pots and pans. Home sweet home. I enrolled Rocky in school; it was conveniently located just across the street. He skipped kindergarten and I put him in first grade.

John started dealing Quaaludes for Geronimo at night. Not surprisingly, he ingested or smoked all the profits and often ended up owing more than he earned. He also became friends with Roy and his wife Flowers, who lived on the other side of town with their five children. Roy, a black man, was an ex-con and had learned to box in prison, which he taught to John in exchange John taught him to scuba dive. Roy, John and Rachel, went diving and spear-fishing together. I was the designated baby sitter, bait cutter and fish cleaner.

In less than three months the house was sold. We had to get out so that the new owners could renovate it and move in. We packed our belongings into the bus and headed up the Keys about 20 miles. While we looked for a permanent place to live, we camped at night at the Sub Pits on Boca Chica Naval Air Station, along with numerous other vagabonds. We'd all party there at night with campfires, swimming, music and dancing. During the day, we'd spend time on one the many local Key West beaches.

The Sub Pits were deep canals cut into the coral, used for submarines during wartime. The water was clean and clear. Dive shops used them for certifying divers. Rocky and Lavina learned to swim there. It was tons of fun!

You had to be careful during high tides or you could get stranded on the thin strip of road between the pits. The water would wash over the sides of the canals and you could easily drive right in to one of the canals – you could see cars that had driven off the edge at the bottom of the canals. At night, when water covered the road, maneuvering the road became quite a feat. Once, water came half-way up the wheels on the bus.

We finally settled in to Lazy Lakes Campground on Sugarloaf Key. Reasonably priced, with showers, a rec room, pool tables and ping pong, it was a neat place to camp. The salt water lakes were great for swimming and fishing, and there were lots of other kids around. I enrolled Rocky in Sugarloaf Elementary school. The bus stop was at the entrance of the campground.

We had installed a propane stove, sink and cabinets in the bus. We tinted the windows, put curtains on them and made another curtain to divide the sleeping area from the front of the bus. Home sweet home.

We even bought a car for traveling back and forth to Key West. John and Rachel worked at Geronimo's shop until summer when the season was over. I got a job driving for Five 6's taxi in Key West. I worked four 12-hour days and was making fifty to one-hundred dollars in cash a day. Rachel watched the kids while I was working.

John and Geronimo went to Mexico for a drug deal. There, they packed two suitcases full of pot and two drugged parrots. Geronimo crossed back into the U.S. in the car, leaving John to take a bus from Oaxaca to the border with the suitcases. Somehow, John lost track of the suitcases. I had to send him money to get a bus ticket to Key West, and to get food and stay in a motel until the suitcases showed up. Believe it or not, the suitcases did show up with none of the contents disturbed. After getting to the border, he waded across the Rio Grande, suitcases and all, then found the bus station and headed for Key West.

He arrived two days later looking pretty wild. We got him home, unpacked the stash and resuscitated the parrots. All was well. I prayed for John the whole time he was gone. Who knew God was so gracious and so patient? Who knew He had such love and care for the foolhardy? Would I ever learn?

John became friends with one of Geronimo's business partners, Jim, who was from Detroit. He invited us to come up and stay with him until things got back to normal in the Keys. It was 1980 and the Mariel Boat Lift was in progress, throwing local life into pandemonium. The streets of Key West were lined with every size and make of boat imaginable as the owners waited their turn to get in the water and head to Cuba to bring back refugees.

Men, women and children were everywhere, waiting to be processed by the immigration service. Prisoners and mental patients were dealt with first, transported by busloads to detention camps. Camps were set up to provide shelter for women and children until they could be picked up by relatives. There was good money in it all, especially for boat owners and taxi drivers, but after a few weeks, it was getting to be too much.

Rachel, Lavina and Snow flew to Detroit with Lisa, a friend of Jim's. She had a nice apartment, where there was room for us to stay. John, Jim, Rocky and I drove the trip in the bus. Traveling with John was not always pleasant, but this jaunt was a little bit better since Jim kept John distracted from constantly picking on us.

We stayed in the party mode the whole time we were in Detroit – dropping acid, smoking pot and snorting cocaine every day. We also introduced ourselves to crack. We attended a Fleetwood Mac concert high as kites and decked out in our finest, with our handmade jewelry dripping off us. We were pretty sure we looked like we were among the famous.

One night when we were all tripping, Rachel and I realized John and Lisa were having an affair. He asked her to become another one of his wives. I was so high, all I could do was laugh and think how ridiculous it was that she would even consider it. After eight years of John's constant affairs, I thought it was as sad as it was amusing. She was going for it, and I so wanted to tell her what a mistake she was making and how hard it would be – but I didn't dare. I also knew Rachel would make her life a living hell.

Lisa got kicked out of her apartment due to our noisy, late-night partying and the overcrowded conditions. We then rented a house in Grosse Ile for the summer. Sleeping arrangements were getting difficult with one more adult and another child on board. If there was any intimacy going on, it was by appointment. Not very romantic, but John was in his heyday.

All too often, I got left behind to do the babysitting, including Lisa's son, which I resented. I didn't particularly enjoy parading around for everyone to see what our lifestyle was all about, so I was embarrassed, angry and feeling left out – all at once. Still, incapable of either leaving or speaking up for myself. Messed up.

Out of frustration and unhappiness, I went to Cleveland by bus for a few days. The visit was short and I told my mom everything was great and we had all we needed. A lie, of course, but I was afraid to say more. Still, I was anxious to get back for fear I was missing out on a party or concert and because I wanted to know what was going on with everyone. I was pregnant again and should have been thinking first of the welfare of the kids. Lisa was pregnant by this time, too.

What kinds of life was this? Man, oh man.

Chapter 11
It's Out There Somewhere

My input never carried much weight. "We" usually meant John, since he just did whatever he wanted to do. Or, whatever he and Rachel wanted. That said, in July, we decided to head back to the Florida Keys. I'm not really sure why, but probably because we didn't pay the rent and got booted from the house. So much for summer in Grosse Ile.

We didn't think the bus would make the trip back, so I signed up for a drive-away van and put the bus in storage. The van was totally empty inside and brand new. We stuffed our clothes and some mattresses inside, loaded up all eight of us and hit the road. We arrived in Key West mid-August, when it was as hot and humid as it could be, and the mosquitoes and no-see-ums were at their worst. We bought a tent and set up home at a campground. We chose a site with electricity so we could have a fan to keep the mosquitoes at bay; it was that or be eaten alive. Bug spray alone was useless.

We crammed all of us into the tent and it started raining. And raining. And raining. We couldn't run the fan because we'd be electrocuted. We put the flaps down to keep the rain out, but then it seeped in under the tent. Our foam rubber mattresses just soaked up the water. Basically, they became hot, soggy sponges. The worst camping experience ever!

It got even worse. John and I had to return the van to central Florida, so we left Lisa, Rachel and the kids to fend for themselves. The plan was to get our deposit back, buy a cheap car and drive back to the Keys that same day. Easy-peasy, right? Wrong.

First, the van had a few scratches and the company was not too happy about that. As usual, I, with my sweet face, had to play the front man and deal with it alone. John couldn't show his face in dealings with the public or he would likely have been arrested just on general principles. The return took all day and it was too late to get anything else done, so we checked into a motel. John wanted to get intimate, but the day's drama left me completely out of the mood.

As usual, John got what he wanted. I was so shy and insecure, even after being with him for years, that I couldn't say no, even though I wanted to. I was such a mess, and I had begun to see this more clearly than ever just before we left Michigan with the addition of another wife and her child.

The next day, John and I finally bought another wreck of a car and headed back to the Keys. We arrived to the same torrential rains with stifling heat and humidity. Rachel, Lisa and the kids were huddled in the tent, soaking wet and trying to run a fan without getting shocked. Certainly, Lisa was getting a glimpse of what lay ahead.

I have no doubt Rachel was less than gracious toward Lisa and her son while John and I were gone. Lisa really hung onto John after that. I felt guilty for leaving them in those wretched conditions while we were up in relatively cooler and drier air. We tried staying the night in the tent and the car, but we were all miserable and restless. The next day, we headed into Key West to make some money. There we were, eight bodies with all our clothes and gear stuffed into a sedan, stewing in the excruciating heat and humidity. Not fun.

We made a little money selling jewelry and pot, enough to rent a U-Haul trailer, and then headed out of the heat and humidity, westward bound. We traveled as far as we could, then pawned, sold or traded whatever we could for gas, food and motel money. At one point, we traded a TV for about $20 in gas. Lisa's TV, by the way. Right there at the gas pump, we had to unload most of the trailer to get to the TV. Truly, we were livin' the dream.

We used the gas station restroom to wash up and change clothes before getting back on the road. We were somewhere in Alabama when the car's transmission began to go out. We limped into a used car dealer and traded that wreck for another wreck. We hitched the trailer to it and got right back on the road.

While we weren't in the extreme heat and humidity of the Keys any longer, we were traveling through the summer heat of the deep south. Three women, two of us pregnant, four unhappy kids, and one husband. Tempers began to flare, especially between the women, and the kids were cranky and restless. We were stuck with one another.

We finally made it to New Mexico and camped at Tommy Lee's place in China Springs. At this point, Rachel made her move against Lisa. She forced John to turn her out for too much whining and a child who was not liking one moment of our adventurous lifestyle. Lisa had been with us for only about six weeks and she was on her way with a car, some money and pregnant, to find some relatives she had in Texas.

That left the rest of us stuck where we were with a U-Haul trailer but no transportation – a trailer that was supposed to have been returned in Florida. Tommy, gracious man that he was, let us stay while we finagled for another car and enough money to get us to California. We weren't very successful.

I was so anxious to move on that I volunteered to go to Tucson and find a drive-away car that would get us there. I took a bus by myself with some of our Navajo blankets and jewelry I could pawn to raise money we needed.

I wasted no time getting to the drive-away company to fill out the paperwork so I could get back to Gallup as soon as possible; I didn't like my children being so far away. There was one small hitch – the only car the company had was supposed to be delivered to New Jersey! Clever criminal that I had become, I lied and said that was exactly where I was headed.

I picked up the car the next morning, even though I was hot, tired, discouraged and really nervous they'd find out about my lie. I remember praying that I'd make it through and that my kids would be okay. I drove straight through to Gallup, seven to eight hours. The kids were fine; Tommy Lee had looked after them. Why, I didn't know, but God made sure I made it through and that the kids were okay.

The following day, we hitched up the trailer, said our goodbyes to Tommy, Irene and his family, crammed ourselves into the car and took off. I have no doubt that Tommy prayed for us that day and had been praying for us since he rescued us from that blizzard a few years back. He was truly a man of God.

We arrived in Northern California several days later, at the Round Valley Reservation where Rachel's family lived. It is a very remote area, just a small valley in the hills on a winding road, 50 miles from the nearest larger town. We stayed with her brother and sister-in-law and their four kids. We unloaded the trailer and hid it on the reservation but continued to drive the car around.

Rachel's brother had just harvested some homegrown pot, so John and Rachel were helping him to get it ready to sell. The kids were all outside playing in the front yard. I headed into the house as Rachel's sister-in-law headed out, on her way to the store in their pickup truck. The kids knew she was headed to the store, so they climbed into the back to ride along.

As she started to leave, not able to see our little one, she backed over two-year old Snow, running over her head and chest. The kids all came running back inside screaming, and we ran out to find her lying under the truck. John pulled her out. I took her and sat with her in my arms while someone called 911. The tire had scraped away the skin from her right temple, exposing the bone. Her chest and right arm were scraped and bleeding.

I was terrified; Snow was in shock. I rode with her in the ambulance to the nearest hospital, 50 miles down the mountain. They took one look at her and sent her on to the next town where there was a bigger hospital. She was taken directly to surgery. They cleaned and bandaged her wounds and stitched up the skin on the side of her face. She stayed about a week and I stayed with her, sleeping on a cot.

My baby was traumatized, but she was alive. Only the Lord knows how much I prayed for her. When we were finally back home, I didn't let her out of my sight. It took almost a year for her to get back to normal. I was made to feel that it was all my fault because I was watching the children. Rachel's sister-in-law felt awful, too. I didn't want to stay there anymore, but we stayed about another month. Then we headed to the coast for a few days. I was five months pregnant.

As we drove up the coast, we came across a house for rent. We turned into the driveway to take a look. It was empty and no one was around. We found an unlocked window and had Rocky climb in and open the front door so we could look around. It was a really nice A-frame house, fully carpeted, with three bedrooms, two baths, a fireplace and spiral staircase leading to the second floor.

We called the real estate company, and I'll never know how or why, but they rented it to us. We moved in the following week. It was pure heaven. Rocky and Lavina got signed up for school. We set up a silver shop in the downstairs bedroom and found a store in town that bought jewelry from us. Finally! Things were looking up; it seemed as if we were back on track to our dream.

Soon, John got stopped for a broken taillight in the car that was long since supposed to have been delivered to New Jersey. He was arrested for driving a stolen car with stolen plates. The police got my name from the drive-away company in Tucson and they took me in for questioning. I was fingerprinted, but I don't remember what I told them or even if I said anything at all.

It turned out that the car's owner had died and his relatives didn't want to press charges; they just wanted the car back. Once again, there we were, dancing with danger. And once again, there was God keeping us out of danger. I didn't even thank Him. I don't think I ever did during all those years. I was oblivious to the fact that He loved me and loved me a lot.

Sonny, was born in March on Friday the 13th no less. My fourth home birth. He was a hefty baby, probably more than eight pounds.

I started a garden that spring and we had ducks and chickens. Snow was doing much better and

made two of the chickens her pets, naming them
Brenda and Barbara.

Life was good.

Chapter 12
What Now?

Yes, life was good. Until we were asked to move out the following October. This time, not our fault! The owners wanted to move one of their relatives into the house. I started searching for a new home and put a free ad on a local radio show describing what we were looking for. Lo and behold, we got a call from a young couple who said they had the perfect place for us.

It was about 30 miles north, right off the highway on about 30 acres with a river running through it, private beach access, and forest all around. It was a two-story block structure, a former bar, with three bedrooms, a bath, a kitchen and a front room, all upstairs; the downstairs was one large open room. The price was low and there was even a greenhouse! Everything we were looking for and more, almost too good to be true.

We found out the couple had just made a lot of money from growing pot on the property and wanted to leave as soon as possible for fear of being caught. That explained a lot. We lived there for more than a year when the sky fell. Federal agents showed up and posted notice that the property was being confiscated as part of a drug raid. We had two weeks to get out. Too good to be true, all right – not to mention that but for the grace of God, it could have easily been us with the Feds on our back.

We scrambled trying to figure out what to do. John finally decided to send me and the kids to Ohio to stay with my Mom while he and Rachel drove our recently purchased cargo van back to Key West. They were joined by a biker couple, Lobo and Noreen, and their Harley rode along in the back of the van.

I bought tickets for me and the four kids from a newspaper ad. We got a ride to San Francisco, about 200 miles away, with a couple we knew. When we got there, I was to meet the people at the airport to get the tickets. This went fine, but when I presented the vouchers, the airline would not accept them because they were not in my name. There I stood in the middle of the airport with four kids, ages 2, 5, 8 and 11, and our baggage, but no tickets. Alone and holding the bag, once again. What now?

Somehow, I remembered the phone number of the people who sold me the tickets; I called them and told them what was going on. Thank God, they were honorable and came back to the airport and made sure we got our tickets. Thank God, for sure – only He could have pulled that one off. The trip was long and exhausting and we arrived in Cleveland late in the evening.

My brother was supposed to pick us up at the airport but couldn't make it at the last minute. His friends, who lived close to the airport, picked us up and took us to their house. They also fed us and gave us a bed for the night. The next day my brother picked us up and took us to Mom's house. She welcomed us with open arms, gave us shelter, and loved us. I probably have never mentioned her name – Fortunata Grace – and she always lived up to it.

My sister and her husband lived with Mom, and both of them were completely gracious, although I felt we were encroaching on their space. My sister was pregnant, due in February. It was September, so I enrolled Rocky and Lavina in school. We qualified for welfare and food stamps. I made beadwork to sell at craft shows, and Mom let me use her car whenever I needed it. Life really was looking up, for me and for the kids. But I was not satisfied – still restless. I wanted to be back with John and Rachel.

When I talked with them on the phone it seemed they weren't very anxious for me to return. They said they didn't have a place for us to stay, not a particularly new challenge – I think they were just having too much fun. They were living here and there, most likely doing coke, and hanging out with the other druggies. I was missing out! Here I was, with a clear opportunity to make a better choice for me and for the kids. But no, I was adamant about us getting back with John and Rachel.

I had made arrangements to take part in a big craft show at a Jewish community center. I was on my way to making my own money with my crafts. Instead, when I got my welfare check and food stamps, I bought tickets for me and the kids to fly to Miami. I packed what we had and got my brother to drive me to the airport. That was that.

When we arrived in Miami there was no way that John could pick us up, so we took Greyhound to Key West, arriving early the next morning. I can't remember doing this with four kids and all our luggage, which seems odd to me now. Once we arrived at the Key West bus station, John had not yet arrived to pick us up. So, we sat in the hot sun until he and Rachel showed up. They seemed happy to see the kids but didn't have any idea how or where we would live. I didn't care. I just wanted to be there with them. I didn't consider anything else – I just wanted what I wanted.

We camped wherever we could stay a while for free, sometimes going to Sugarloaf Key to camp at Lazy Lakes. John got a construction job. We would drive him to work in the morning, meet him there at lunch to bring him food, then pick him up at quitting time. In between, we would go to one beach or another, do laundry, go shopping or take the kids to a playground.

102

We eventually bought another extended van which we used for all the back and forth trips, leaving the cargo van at the campground. It gave us more sleeping room. We got on a list for public housing; when a two-bedroom unit opened up, we took it until a three-bedroom unit became available. I got a job as a waitress at a Holiday Inn, and soon got Rachel a job there making salads and desserts. I worked the breakfast/lunch shift and banquets.

Rachel was working with me at a banquet when she hurt her back. Worker's Compensation sent her to the doctor and paid her for her time off. She went to the doctor for heat treatments and pills but wasn't getting better. Her Worker's Comp benefits were cut off, so we used the services of a lawyer who agreed to take the case pro bono. She sued and finally won two years later.

While we lived there, Snow celebrated her sixth birthday and Sonny his third. Lavina was nine and Rocky, 12. I continued to work at the hotel, and moved to the dinner shift, which paid more in tips. We became friends with Louis, a Cuban man, and his wife and two sons; he and John met at the construction site. They went lobster diving and spear fishing together, so we ate like kings. They also liked to smoke pot and do lines of coke together, and of course, Rachel and I joined in.

I worked at the hotel for about three years – enough to earn a week's paid vacation, my first ever! I used it to go to Cleveland to celebrate my mom's 75th birthday and retirement from Sears, Roebuck & Co. John quit the construction job because he kept getting skin infections from the coral dust and cement. He began dealing again and driving taxi third shift. I hardly ever saw him since he slept when I was at work. He would spend a little time with the kids, then leave for work when I got home.

Rocky, Lavina and Snow were enrolled in school, so I didn't get to see them much, either. Rachel watched them most of the time. Why I didn't realize this was a terrible mistake I'll never know. Rachel's ideas about raising children were less than ideal.

Her motto was "What doesn't kill you will make you stronger". She detested what she perceived as weakness. One of her go-to actions was to heat up a butter knife and ask the kids a question, getting them to stick out their tongue. Then she'd ask the question, telling them that if they told the truth, they wouldn't get burned, but if they lied, they would get burned. Also, she liked to whip them with a green switch – barely okay, even when you do it only rarely. But she was into leaving marks on their legs and butt. She would do this in front of me and threaten to tell John if I interfered.

I learned the worst of it years later. She started molesting Rocky when he was about nine years old. He and I have talked some about it but the wounds are deep. It was years before I learned of it; he was sworn to secrecy for fear he'd be thrown out or killed.

I may never really know the full extent of Rachel's effect on my children – not to mention how our atypical lifestyle might have affected them. Not so much our unusual "marriage", but the drugs, rootlessness, upheaval, contentiousness, criminality, lack of structure and moral direction, and so much more. They all struggle with emotional and stress issues. Who knows, maybe that would have been the outcome anyway.

Then there is the fact that I was so busy making what I thought was a good life for everyone that I didn't spend the quality time with them that I could have and should have. Instead, I let Rachel have way too much of the "mothering", including the discipline.

While John and even Rachel contributed income, even if from questionable sources, over the years I was the one who had regular employment, sometimes juggling two jobs and working at night. But, as far as money was concerned, drugs were the priority, then beer and food, then maybe rent and utilities. My good credit got us loans, and I managed to pay them off, but not without late

105

fees and fines. Then, it was my credit that was in trouble when we couldn't pay at all.

Wherever we were, it was I who took most of the responsibility for the household. Everything. I did the laundry, housecleaning and cooking for eight people. When we had appliances, they were usually inadequate; if we used propane, I was the one who usually made the trip to make sure the tank got refilled. I was so determined to show John and Rachel what a regular family could be. I actually believed I was doing just that.

Our steady stream of junk vehicles needed constant maintenance. If I was able, I did most of the repairs – replacing brakes, doing oil changes, tune-ups and more. At one time, we were able to buy a newer Toyota pick-up truck with a small down payment with money we made from our crafts. It was such a relief to have a reliable vehicle for a while. It didn't last long.

After making a windfall in the pot growing business we decided to trade in the pick-up for a Toyota 4-Runner. It was a great vehicle for us until our son-in-law borrowed it and blew out the transmission. We had no insurance and were still making payments on it. Well, we were supposed to be making payments, but we stopped and just waited for it to be repossessed. That's how we dealt with our problems.

I also did all kinds of home repairs. Replacing the pump in the water well, fixing roof leaks, unplugging drains, snaking out backed-up septic systems, patching leaky pipes, and even electrical work, just to name a few.

I had the babies, nursed and diapered them, and doctored them when they were sick. I was the one who got the kids off to school and made sure they went to sports practice and games. All this while also feeding and caring for horses, dogs or other animals, plus mending fences, tending gardens, orchards and marijuana crops.

I realize I *allowed* all this to happen; I just wanted to achieve our dream and build our dream life. I stuffed my resentments and frustrations, often unable to stand up either for myself or for the kids. It was endlessly stressful. I developed an ulcer at one point, which went untreated for months. How easy it was to see faults in others, but not my own crazy brokenness. I'm pretty sure that even if I had seen it, I wouldn't have had the wisdom or wherewithal to do anything about it. So much for my behavior over the years.

We finally moved into a trailer with a yard on Big Coppitt Key, about seven miles north of Key West. We were able to buy a late model Ford Escort station wagon with a loan from a local credit union, thanks to my good employment history. John went to work for Axle, a mason who also owned a gym. Rachel began to work at the gym. We got to work out there for free. I really got into working out and lifting weights; I even entered a local bench press contest and came in second in my weight class.

Then, Axle asked us to grow dope for him in Georgia. His wife owned a few acres there, with a comfortable cabin on it. So, I took a leave of absence from my job, John loaded up the Escort with marijuana starts, and we drove up to the property. No telling what would have happened if we'd been stopped. Once we got there, we stood out – a bunch of hippie types among the local country folk.

Far out, man.

Chapter 13
Snakes

We successfully planted the starts without getting bitten by snakes; we also put in a large, legitimate garden, with tomatoes, peppers, beans, squash and corn. We saw plenty of snakes as we worked – which was creepy enough – but it was the snakes we didn't see that scared us the most. We met up with a local farmer who had cows and horses, a great source of free fertilizer! So, we lined the station wagon with heavy-gauge black plastic and brought back several loads of manure for the gardens.

John decided to go back to Florida to bring the rest of the family to Georgia so we would all be together. This left me alone at the cabin to watch over the gardens with no phone, TV or radio. I did have his pistol, though, and food.

I still had plenty to do. During the day, I worked the garden then climbed the hill to tend the plants in the other garden. In the evening, I read or played solitaire on the porch. It was summer, so the days were generally sunny and hot. The nights, still and starry.

One afternoon, when I was resting from the heat on the front porch, I noticed smoke rising in the distance. It increased more and more as I watched. Then, I saw a pickup truck racing from the direction of the fire and it soon passed right in front of me. I decided to walk to the nearest neighbors, an older couple, to see if they had any idea about the source of the smoke. They investigated, and finding that another neighbor's house was on fire, they called the fire department. The fire crew arrived but not before the place was destroyed; they determined it was arson.

The fire department came to the cabin later and took my statement about the truck I'd seen fleeing the scene. I was hesitant, but knew I needed to tell the truth. The next day, the Sheriff's deputies showed up. It scared me a little bit at first, but they only wanted me to accompany them to see if I could pick out the men I saw leaving the scene of the fire. They drove me though the part of town they believed the men lived, but I couldn't make a positive I.D. After that, I took John's loaded pistol with me wherever I went and slept with it near my bed. Sure enough, a few days later a pickup truck with three men in it drove up to the cabin.

I happened to be on the porch reading. Thank God, they didn't get out of the truck, but they did try to get some sort of conversation going. I told them my husband was inside. I slowly reached over and put my hand on the pistol. I don't know if they saw me do that, but they left after saying just a few words. I sometimes wonder what I would have done if they had approached me. After

110

that, I was more guarded than ever. I was always looking up and down the road watching for the dust of an approaching vehicle. You never knew when a snake might show up in those parts!

Finally, John and the rest of the family arrived, albeit a bit battered. I was so relieved and happy to see them! They had been through quite an ordeal, too. John was pulling his boat and trailer with the little four-cylinder station wagon. At one point, the car had a flat tire and swerved as John tried to get it to the side of the road.

As they pulled over, the trailer and boat detached and then overturned onto the highway. Our possessions were inside the boat, so everything – clothes, pots, pans, blankets, etc. – was strewn all over the road. They retrieved what they could and stuffed what would fit into the back of the wagon and moved on, with the four kids sitting on top of it all. The boat and trailer were left behind, a disappointment since we were hoping to take it out on a nearby lake.

After we'd all traded stories about what had happened, we got everyone settled in, fed and off to bed. The next day we looked over the garden and then went up the hillside to check on the progress of the growing pot, and to water and fertilize. We had found a spring nearby, so we filled five-gallon watering cans and carried them down to the plants, always on the lookout for snakes. It was a back-breaking, time-consuming and very tedious routine we followed every other day. The rest of the time was dedicated to the vegetable garden. Drugs always came first!

John made friends with a local farmer who had horses that needed to be trained. He hired John to do it. Meanwhile, I found a job at a shoe factory – tying laces on work boots. The pay was poor and it was hot and smelly. Then I got a job cleaning motel rooms until I was hired by a local restaurant. Tips were meager since it was a buffet in a town of farmers and poor families. But, I got a second job as a waitress at a hotel & restaurant on the main highway that was popular with locals and tourists. I was able to make more money there but was definitely an outsider. I knew I could live with it until the crops came in.

The kids had a great summer while we were in north Georgia. John met a local man who headed a club he called the Wilderness Scouts. He was a nice guy, a Christian man. He had two boys and a girl about the same ages as our kids; they made friends and joined the scouts. They went swimming and to meetings, on campouts, and most likely heard a lot about Jesus. I think he even took them to church quite often.

Axle and his wife Elsie decided to come up from Florida to see how things were going with the crop and the cabin. John made arrangements for transporting the pot back to Florida, then Axle and Elsie left a few days later. On my way down the hill one day while they were there, I apparently brushed up against what was probably some kind of caterpillar that stung me. I didn't see what it was to know for sure. It was like getting an electric shock; it almost knocked me over. I got dizzy almost immediately and had a hard time making it back to the cabin. When I got there I just collapsed on the front porch where we'd put our bed while Axle and Elsie were there. I felt so bad and woozy that I couldn't move off the bed.

John, Rachel, Axle and the kids were all going camping except for Sonny, who was too little to go. Elsie was there, so she was kind enough to look after him while I just lay there and slept until the next day. Once again, it seems that God was watching over me. I recovered completely by the next evening and was up and about again. I now realize that no one else seemed too concerned about me. They just left me there and went off to have a good time. It should have been obvious to me right then that I wasn't worth much to them. I now know it's a good thing that God thinks I am worth something.

When we went up to check on the crop after Axle and Elsie left, we found that a good part of it had been "harvested" by someone else. Thieves, or maybe even the authorities. We weren't sure. We then had to sneak around to all the plots to see if all of it was gone. We only had a few plants left. I guess it was true – it was the snakes you didn't see that were the most dangerous.

It was finally time to return to the Keys. I don't remember the trip back, so it must have been uncharacteristically drama-free. We stayed with Elsie and Axle until I found us another trailer to rent on Big Coppitt Key. I had to convince the owner that there weren't too many of us for the little two-bedroom trailer. I had gotten pretty good at telling the truth only when it suited me.

In most ways, life was rocking along pretty normally for us. Lavina got a puppy from a neighbor; then it got run over and she was heartbroken. Sonny was about 5, for him a very mischievous age. When no one was looking, he got on the boat a friend had docked in the canal behind our trailer. He found a flare gun and shot it off inside the boat. Thank goodness, he wasn't burned and the boat didn't catch on fire. I was 40, and pregnant again. John and Rachel were doing a lot of coke, smoking a lot of pot, and drinking a lot of beer. I joined in, of course, until I knew I was pregnant – then I just smoked pot. As if.

Yep, everything was rocking along pretty normally. John and Rachel were still working for Axle. John was laying brick and Rachel worked at the gym. We all worked out a lot, so maybe that was why John was paying more attention to me than usual

– which made Rachel jealous and spiteful. She started flirting with one of our good neighbors. No telling how far that went, but she and John were getting into lots of huge fights. Rachel also took out some of her animosity on the local coke dealer they used. I'm not sure what he did to cause it, maybe he cheated them somehow, but she went to his house and took a baseball bat to the back window of his car.

Soon after, when we were all in the trailer getting ready for dinner, the dealer drove by and fired some gunshots into the trailer and narrowly missed one of us. Naturally, John and Rachel went after him, John with a gun and Rachel with a crowbar. Rachel liked fighting, remember – she learned everything on the reservation, where you fought or you died. All that seemed to have happened was that Rachel busted out the windshield of the dealer's car with it. We never saw him again! It wasn't clear to me then but it is now: snakes are just about everywhere, not just in the gardens of northeast Georgia.

Meanwhile, I was getting big. I worked driving a taxi and as a waitress until I was about 6 months pregnant. We decided to purchase another school bus. We painted it forest green and called it "The Emerald Express". We parked it in the yard next to the trailer and fixed it up. We made beds, put in a kitchen, got a port-a-potty, tinted the windows, put in storage cabinets and more – all the comforts of home! We had several backyard mechanics helping us with the engine work the bus needed. I was right in there with them, big belly and all. Under the hood, trying to fix the carburetor. I had become a pretty good mechanic over the years. Our plan was to head back to California as soon as the bus was ready.

And head back we did.

Chapter 14
A Few Stops Along the Way

We headed for California even though the bus wasn't quite ready. It was spring of 1987 and I was eight months pregnant. We got as far as central Florida when the bus began to have major problems. We were stuck in the median strip for a day and a half. Several people stopped to see if there was something they could do to help. One of them seemed to know the problem and told us what part we needed. We located a nearby parts store, got the problem fixed and were on our way.

Then, not too much further down the road, the bus had a flat tire and we pulled off on a sandy berm. We didn't have a spare, so we decided that since we still had five good tires, we'd make our way to the next truck stop. But, the bus was now stuck in the sand. We tried everything – we rocked the bus, we put boards under the tires and shoveled the sand away. Yet, all we managed to do was to get the bus deeper into the sand until the tires on the right side of the bus were almost buried.

Then the bus started to tip over. We got everyone out of the bus without delay and tied everything down as best we could. I prayed like crazy. Finally, a man with a large tow truck came by and helped us out. Hmm. My prayers were answered once again. It took more than an hour of winching the bus this way and that before the bus was free. The

117

tow truck driver wouldn't take any money. He probably felt sorry for the kids and me and had a good laugh too. We loaded everyone back onto the bus – but we still had the flat tire to deal with.

We drove only a short way before we saw a large shopping center where we could park the bus and camp overnight. The next day we found a cheap used tire and a place to get the flat changed. We were off again. When we got to Lake Alfred in central Florida, we camped at a flea market, paid a fee and set up our wares. The bus's transmission was still having problems, so we decided to stay there until we could get it fixed. About a week later, we decided to go into town so I could apply for food stamps. John and I had to hitchhike to get there. Right. A strange-looking, long-haired hippie man and his very pregnant woman.

We got plenty of stares and honks, but no ride. So, we walked a long way before some really scary redneck boys picked us up. I couldn't wait to get out of that car! Then, I sat in the food stamp office for hours just to get an appointment. Luckily, I got emergency approval and got the food stamps that day. We bought some groceries which we carried through town to the highway and tried once again to hitch a ride. We walked almost a quarter of the way before some guys in a flatbed pickup truck picked us up. We were grateful but had to hang on for dear life!

It was late afternoon and I started to prepare dinner. I was so exhausted that I decided to lay down for a nap. After about an hour, I woke up and my water broke. The little kids, John and Rachel went to bed around 9 p.m. Rocky stayed up with me, watching television. It was a clear, starry night with just a sliver of a new moon, and thankfully not too hot or humid.

I was in labor for about 7 hours. At the final stage, I woke John and Rachel and got out the birthing kit I had prepared. I got on my knees to give birth, facing an open window for air and holding onto John's shoulders. Our daughter June was born a little after midnight on May 2. She was beautiful, with lots of black hair.

I had somehow managed to stay quiet enough during the birth to not wake or disturb any of the other campers, so until I came outside with the baby, people were surprised she had been born. The flea market manager heard about June's arrival and called the county nurse to check us out. She came and found no problems with me or with June. All was well!

We were stuck at the flea market for the next couple of weeks while the transmission was being fixed. John had befriended a black man who was willing to work on the bus in trade for some of our jewelry and other items. Finally, we were on the road once again, heading out of Florida and westward for California. We stopped at various flea markets along the way to make enough money for food and gas.

By the time we reached Texas, we were limping along on four out of six tires; one of the dual tires on each side of the bus was flat. There we were in the middle of cowboy country looking like a bunch of hippie-types – which made help hard to come by. Finally, a man and his son drove up beside us and asked if we needed some assistance.

He saw the kids, sized up our situation and invited us to follow him to his place so we could rest and get the repairs we needed. He, his wife and several children lived in a trailer in the middle of nowhere, surrounded by barbed wire fences, sagebrush, and rattlesnakes. They welcomed us and gave us food, water and a place to stay. I can only believe they were a Godsend – genuine Christian people, Good Samaritans. Our kids had great fun together and they took our kids along to church and to the fair, as I recall. Rachel was introduced to bingo; she went every chance she could and won some much-needed money.

One day, the weather took a turn for the worse, bringing a tornado warning along with it. The Good Samaritan family tied down their trailer and left to wait out the storm safely with relatives. Foolishly, we stayed put in the bus. Tornados were all throughout the area, and one touched down very near us. The wind was strong, rocking the bus all around. Out of the blue, so to speak, Mr. Good Samaritan showed up, put us all in his car and took us to a motel, getting us out of danger. The damage was minimal and we had our lives. Once again, God appeared to be watching out for us, even though we were anything but watching out for Him.

When the bus was finally ready for travel, the Samaritans gave us a wonderful send-off, serving a big pancake breakfast and packing food for us to take along as we traveled. It seemed like it took days and days to make it across Texas. When we at last crossed the border into New Mexico, we all cheered. We headed towards Gallup and went to see our old friend Tommy Lee and his family, the other generous and loving Christian Samaritans God used to take care of us over the years. We enjoyed a few days with them before finishing our trip to California.

About eight weeks after our road trip began, we arrived in Covelo, California, a small valley town on Rachel's reservation in the hills of Mendocino County. It was almost time for school to start, so we registered Rocky in Covelo High School, Lavina in middle school, and Snow in elementary school; Sonny was about kindergarten age.

A week after school began, all the kids came home with head lice – so all of us ended up with lice, even baby June. We tried every over-the-counter remedy, but to no avail. So, we came up with our own remedy. We all saturated our hair with olive oil, which slowed down or killed the lice so we could comb them out with a louse comb or pick them out by hand. We shaved the boys' heads; the girls had long hair, making the process beyond tedious. The most distressing part was seeing my little 12-week old baby crawling with bugs.

A few more weeks in Covelo was all I could take. The drinking and drugging, the dust, dirt and fighting took its toll. I was determined to leave any way I could with or without John and Rachel. Finally, we fired up the bus and headed for the coast. It was cooler, we'd lived in the area before, and we'd be away from Rachel's relatives. It might as well have been heaven.

We stayed at a state campground for a few days until we heard about a private campground situated halfway between Mendocino and Ft. Bragg. It offered month-to-month rental spaces with electricity, shower and laundry. We settled there and put the kids in Mendocino schools. I applied for food stamps and welfare, and John got a job filleting fish in Ft. Bragg.

Rachel was still negotiating with Unemployment Disability for a settlement from the injury she received at the hotel in the Florida Keys and it was settled before the end of the year. With all that money, we even managed to buy a car.

Life was good.

Chapter 15
Crazy House

When Rachel's worker's compensation settlement came in, we decided to look for a home to buy. At first, we were just looking for a rental when we came upon "the house" in Albion, California, on Albion Ridge Rd. Three-and-one-half miles from the Pacific Ocean, it was a large, rather unusual redwood house on 9.35 acres and in need of a lot of repairs. Constructed entirely of redwood 2x6's, it was likely built by several sets of people at different times. It was unique, to say the least. I guess that's what made it our house as no other house could be. Over 2000 square feet of pure crazy!

We moved in September of 1987.

The great room was on the main floor which had a vaulted ceiling and two steps down was the family room which had a wood circular staircase going up to bedrooms. One of the bedrooms had a door that led to the porch roof and another doorway about two feet off the floor which led to another bedroom on the third floor.

That third-floor room had a doorway that led to a loft-of-sorts which overlooked the great room. Another stairway led down to a landing where there was another door that opened to the outside wrap-around porch. Except that it opened about three feet above the floor of the porch deck. So, like many other doors in the house, that door had no real purpose. Those stairs then continued down to the great room.

The kitchen, on the same level as the great room, was narrow and long. Behind it was a bedroom with a doorway to the porch. The bathroom was in the hallway, which led to yet another bedroom which also had a door to the porch. There was also a lower level which had a one-bedroom apartment that consisted of a front room, small kitchen, bathroom and bedroom. There was another level two steps down which was basically a dirt room under the house with the water heater and all the plumbing for the house.

The fun really started when, helped by Rachel's brother, we tore down a wall to open up the kitchen; we had no idea what we were doing – it turned out to be a load-bearing wall. So, we cut down a tree and used that to brace the floor joist. Clever, huh? Not. Then, we put in a sliding glass door on the corner wall, also without proper bracing. We opened up the wall that separated the kitchen from the family room, exposing wiring which was never dealt with properly. It's a wonder it all didn't just collapse in on us.

Then, we decided to move the entire kitchen to the family room and use the former kitchen area as a dining room, taking out the bedroom wall to make one large room. We installed a restaurant-style stainless steel sink and counter bought at a yard sale. The plumbing was never right. We had to cut into the water line to get water to the sink; that meant welding copper piping and matching the drain to the existing PVC drain pipes. Everything leaked, everywhere, always.

We fueled our propane stove with a five-gallon tank that sat on the porch. It was hooked to the stove via a pipe run through a hole cut in the wall. John built the rest of the counters and a table. There were open shelves, not cabinets, for the dishes and food. We also put in extra-wide sliding glass doors facing the north and looking out onto the horse pasture. We were also lucky that wall didn't collapse, because, like the wall we tore down and the other glass doors we put in, we didn't put any proper bracing in place. It was all a real mess.

The fun continued. John decided he didn't like either of the stairways, so he tore them out and rebuilt them – if you want to call it that. He got rid of the one that led to the master bedroom and loft. Instead, he made it run from the front room floor straight up to the loft, taking out the landing. The stairs were slanted and the risers were different heights. He also got rid of the circular staircase and replaced it with a staircase we bought secondhand. It turned out to be a little too short, so John built an extra step at the top to make it fit. Don't bother to wonder if the staircase was safe when it was complete. Nothing John ever built was safe or complete.

Behind the scenes, the plumbing and electrical desperately needed to be redone. The copper pipes were disintegrating and springing leaks everywhere. I jerry-rigged a "temporary" fix by cutting and attaching rubber hoses with hose clamps. Because of the high rust content in the well water, we had to change out rusted water heaters several times. I constantly made so-called improvements on the bathroom sink and tub, which both leaked nonstop; also, the handles rusted off, so we solved that by using vice grips to turn the water on and off. Marginally clever solutions like that were our specialty.

We also had fun with the wrap-around porch. The overhang on the south side leaked unmercifully. I found some used plywood and borrowed a neighbor's ladder and attempted to fix it. I also found some tar paper and tar and tried to seal it. Then I cleaned out the gutters and hoped for the best. The rains came, the seal worked for a short time, then began leaking worse than it had to begin with! Inside, I tried paint, wallpaper and new linoleum flooring over rotted plywood. I tried

127

to replace pieces of plywood with scrap wood I found around the property, but it was like trying to force jigsaw puzzle pieces into places they didn't belong.

I constantly dreamed of making the house run on solar power, but like the remodeling and repairs, that idea pretty much went up in smoke. Pun intended.

Somehow, we never seemed to have enough money to have any of the work done by professionals – even though we always had enough for plenty of dope. We struggled to pay the mortgage each month and had a balloon payment coming up.

I was working evenings as a server at a nearby restaurant-inn and made great money. But, drugs were always the priority, from the start of the day until the end of the day. As hard as I tried to put some of my earnings away for the lean times, I usually got talked out of it so we could have pot or buy munchies at the local store. Money just flowed through our fingers like water; the leaky plumbing in our house was nothing compared to it!

I think it was about 3 years after we started living in the house, the first balloon payment came due. We were somehow able to refinance the house and make the payment. However, our mortgage payment went from $400 to $800 per month.

128

Yikes! John and Rachel were working at a horse ranch, but even with all of us working, we were barely making enough to support our house payment and other expenses plus our voluminous drug use.

About that same time, my job at the restaurant was coming to an end because the restaurant was closing down. I got a job busing tables at another restaurant/resort closer to home, but I'd have to wait a year to qualify to wait tables. John wanted me to quit, but I persevered while we worked to get our jewelry business going.

We acquired several horses over the years, mostly from owners who no longer wanted them. John had Shasta, an Arabian; Rosie, a thoroughbred, and Candy, a hackney pony, were Snow's. Rudy the Appaloosa belonged to Rachel. We also had two ponies.

It usually fell to me to feed and water the horses twice a day, which included giving them alfalfa, grass and an oat/psyllium seed mixture when we had it – plus any vitamins or medicines they might need at the time. It was also up to me to get the feed. That meant either going to the feed store 30 miles away or having the hay delivered when we had the money.

All the children were accomplished riders. Rocky and Lavina worked with John and Rachel at the horse ranch, leading trail rides. Snow excelled with horses. She was only about 15 but competed in the hunter/jumper category in horse shows and on a vaulting team and entered long distance races. She was great when teaching young children to ride. She taught riding to 4H-ers and conducted private lessons to earn money.

Eventually, the house was falling apart on us because of the shoddy materials and workmanship. It was supposed to be our dream house, but in fact, the house was a disaster, and probably dangerous. Even the man who inspected the house before we bought it said the house was dilapidated. We walked, eyes wide closed, into this disaster. I can't believe how stupid we were. It amazing that we survived at all.

We lived in that house for 11 years. Those were the years that I worked the hardest at showing John and Rachel what real family life could be. I wanted to give them that more than anything else. In addition to working evenings, doing regular house cleaning, repairs and upkeep, we also planted several gardens and fruit trees, which I maintained. I grew organic herbs for natural medicinal use and sold culinary herbs to local restaurants.

I worked 4 to 11 p.m. and was home during the day. John and Rachel worked during the day until we got our jewelry business going. Then, they usually worked all night on jewelry and slept during the day. They were sometimes gone to shows several days at a time.

I was up at 6 a.m. to get the kids off to school, lunches and all. I cared for and fed all our horses, dogs, cats, rabbits, chickens and ducks, and the purebred miniature dachshunds we raised and sold. There was food-shopping and cooking for all of us, constant laundry, trips to town to keep the propane tank filled and animal feed stocked. I'd head out for work at 4 p.m., after the kids got home from school. My shift ended at 11 p.m. and I'd head home and fall into bed. Then, I'd get up the next morning and do it all again. Even though I was always considered the weak link in our relationship, not tough enough to "handle it".

I think I was so busy trying to prove myself that I just couldn't see that our crazy, dilapidated house was a metaphor for my whole life. Somehow, I'd walked into the relationship with John and Rachel, eyes wide closed, only to spend years working myself silly trying to fix the leaks, repair the holes, and look past the rust and rot of our so-called relationship to convince myself all was well. Like my constant hope that we'd one day convert the house to solar power, I continued to believe we were working toward our dream. Yet here it was, 20 years later and our life in that house was probably the closest we ever got to it.

Hardly a dream. More like a pipe dream.

Chapter 16
Seeking, Changing

A few months after we moved into the house, our baby June, almost 1 year old, was infected with poison oak, especially around her face and mouth. We were not sure how she contacted it, maybe from someone's clothing or from the dog. It was awful. As it was healing it left scabs on her face which thankfully didn't leave any scars. However, a week or two later she started to have a hard time breathing. We had no idea what was causing it. She also developed a swelling on her neck which I supposed was swollen glands. Finally, after trying every home remedy I could and she just got worse, we took her to the ER.

They tried to x-ray her neck but it was too hard to get a such a young child to drink the barium from a bottle when she had never been fed a bottle before. They did a sonogram instead. They discovered a large mass in her neck and opted to send her immediately by ambulance to University Hospital in San Francisco. I rode with her, and she was taken to surgery as soon as we arrived. She was admitted to the hospital and I stayed with her there for the next 10 days.

The surgeon told me afterwards that they drained a grapefruit-sized mass from her neck which was pressing on her esophagus and causing the breathing difficulty. They administered saline and antibiotics via a tube put in near her collarbone. She also had a tube coming out of her neck where they did the surgical incision to drain the wound; both stayed in the entire 10 days. I continued to breast-feed her in the hospital but had to be very careful not to tug on the tubes.

They moved us to three different rooms during our stay. I had no money with me and only one change of clothes. The hospital staff was wonderful; they brought meals for June so I could eat the solid foods and feed her the soft ones. Because we were in the children's ward, there was a shower and laundry available for parents. What a blessing. June celebrated her first birthday in the hospital. She took her first steps in the halls of the ward with IV tubes and a caddy holding the saline bag rolling down the hall with her.

About the seventh day there, I decided to venture outside for some fresh air while June was napping. I had no idea where I was or which direction to walk. I walked for about a block in both directions and then returned. I didn't know anyone in the city so eventually I called my mother. Once again, she came to my rescue. She sent me money so I could buy food and a gift for June and have money when she was released from the hospital. When we left the hospital, I relied on strangers to direct me to the city bus that would take us to the Greyhound station. I had to find my own way on every leg of our journey home.

Carrying the baby and a bag of items the hospital gave me, I finally arrived at the Greyhound station only to find I had a 3 to 4 hour wait until the bus left. Again, with help from strangers, I got on a local bus and took June to the aquarium to pass the time, then made my way back to the Greyhound station in time to catch my bus to Santa Rosa. There, I had to transfer to a smaller bus to Ukiah and from there, yet another bus to Albion. After arriving there, we had to wait for a while until someone finally came to get us. I sure was glad to be home and with all my children.

During the years in the house, we spent a good amount of time with Rachel's family. They would come to visit us for days at the time. They would go to the ocean to gather seaweed and hunt for abalone on the rocks. And, we would go visit with them on the reservation.

We attended many Indian Brush Dances, also called Round Dances, because a brush fence was put up in a large circle around the dirt dancing area. There was usually a shaman present to perform ritual healing ceremonies, and a sweat lodge used by the dancers to purify themselves prior to the ceremony.

Sometimes, the kids and I were invited to join the dancing. John, besides being white, was not well liked, so he never took part. The women and girls wore long skirts and the men wore ribbon shirts which were handmade with raglan sleeves and colorful ribbons sewn on as fringe. Our kids wore our handmade deerskin moccasins and clothing.

Once or twice, Rachel and John attended a Sun Dance in Arizona, along with one or two of the kids. Outlawed in most states, the Sun Dance ritual featured men who pierced their back or chest and inserted sticks into the cut. Then, ropes with a buffalo skull attached at the end would be tied on to the sticks.

The men then danced in a circle until the skin broke – the goal of the dance. Sometimes a child would sit on the skull to make it heavier. In another version, the men would attach the ropes to a wooden cross, brace their feet on the cross and pull back as hard as they could until the skin around the skin tore, causing them to fall to the ground.

They performed this ritual while fasting for three days, going in and out of the sweat lodge and drinking peyote tea. Their actions were considered a sacrifice to honor The Great Spirit and usually included prayer and visions. Sometimes women and girls took part, cutting pieces of flesh from their arm as their way to honor The Great Spirit.

I never witnessed either of these rituals, mostly because I was not invited and I had a job, but Rocky and Lavina did. No surprise - they weren't too fond of it. One time, Rachel collapsed from dehydration, which really scared them.

What the consequences of events like these and our overall lifestyle might have on us never much crossed my mind. I had my hands full and had no time or inclination to think about it. The kids seemed content. Never mind that I left them with Rachel in charge a lot, even though I thought her approach to child-rearing was pretty odd. Ha!

Little did I realize that things were about to blow completely apart. I was deep into all my self-imposed busyness, complaining about being the one always left at home and hardly ever spending time with John. Out of all this, the secret so-called "relationship" between Rocky and Rachel came to light. There had been clues that went right over my head.

It had dawned on me that, for about a month, Rachel had been acting more oddly than usual. She began smoking cigarettes and showing odd and outward affection for my son. Rocky, who was now 17 and starting his senior year in high school, began spending as much time as he could away from home; he later explained that he was trying not to get cornered. He knew it was wrong and wanted it to end. In fact, he never wanted it to start. But, the abuse had begun when he was a small boy and had very little say one way or the other.

Once the truth came out, Rachel took off for the reservation, drinking and doing who knows what. Rocky stayed away as much as he could to avoid running into John. All the while, John was working on convincing me to not call the authorities to report the abuse. One evening, after talking about the revelations, John made it very clear that he would do about anything to get Rachel back home. He asked me if it was okay for him to ask her to get married. I was numb and still in shock over the whole thing. I said I didn't care and that he should do whatever he wanted. I reluctantly gave my blessing; I hardly know why it even mattered to him what I thought.

Looking back on the situation after all these years I have come to realize that Rachel was laden with guilt and regret but did not know how to get free. She needed a savior and John decided that he was the one. An insufficient one, for sure. As I came to understand later, only Jesus Christ could fill that role with all sufficiency. John then proceeded to lay all the guilt on Rocky.

John and Rachel were soon married in our home by a local minister with our kids, Rachel's family members, and even Rocky in attendance. Fool that I was, not only did I give my blessing to this union, but I also planned the wedding, prepared a huge wedding dinner, made and decorated the wedding cake, and set up the honeymoon cottage on our property. I was more than a fool; I was stupid and blind. It was as if I were in some dream, watching all this from the sidelines as they exchanged vows and rings. Not only was I a fool, stupid and blind, I was also quite high. That was the only way I could make it through all this. My state of mind was in a very bad place.

Not long after that, in 1989, Rocky graduated from high school. I made arrangements for him to spend the summer with my mother in Ohio until he started college in the fall. He worked to earn money for school, then came home with just enough time to pack his things and leave again. John, Rachel and I drove him there.

I don't know why they had to go; I figure they wanted to be sure he was gone and to let him know he was no longer a part of the family. They blamed him for the illicit relationship with Rachel, saying that he took advantage of Rachel's "instability". Lame, lame, lame. They tried to cut me off from him at every turn, continually telling me he was no good, evil, and a troublemaker. Worst of all, they succeeded in convincing the

139

other kids to have nothing to do with him; they have almost no relationship to this day.

Yet, true to form, I took all this passively on the outside while seething with hurt, anger and defeat inside myself. There were long periods of time where Rocky and I had no contact. I only called him when no one else was around. I managed to visit him two or three times in his four years at college but made sure to see him graduate. We now have a great relationship. He teaches high school math and has been happily married for well over 20 years.

It didn't take long after Rocky headed off to college for it all to catch up with me. I had hardly recognized the emotional pain I had been experiencing. I was depressed and having thoughts of suicide. One day, I opened a bottle of wine and starting drinking and added smoking pot to that. Then I decided to drop some acid, actually believing it would help me think things through. I didn't want the kids to see me in such a state, so I went down to the cabin to be alone.

I was very high and started to feel really good. I was listening to music, dancing around and smoking pot to keep the edge off. I was sure that once John got home, he'd come down to find me and that we would talk and make love – neither of which had happened in a long time. Wrong. He didn't show up; instead, he had Rachel call me to come up for dinner. I was crushed. I decided I'd wait him out, but he never came. I finally gave in and dragged myself up with my tail between my legs. I was nothing to him, nor to the others. I felt worthless, powerless and completely alone.

From then on, I knew John did not care about me, and probably never had. Nothing made much sense anymore. I found myself searching, I guess for some peace or something to believe in. I read books about I Ching, White Magic and astrology. I wanted a purpose, and of all things, forgiveness. Can you imagine? After all the years of believing I was living my purpose and pursuing our dream! And forgiveness for what, anyway? I always did the right thing, keeping the family together with precious little help from John or Rachel.

Then came the summer of 1993. One day I was working in the garden, and when I came in, Rachel was watching TV. A Christian evangelist was on, and somehow, he got my attention. He was talking about Jesus and the Cross and being "born again". I didn't understand much, but what he had to say set off bells in my head – and my heart. I somehow knew he was telling the truth. I think deep down Rachel was also affected by this evangelist, but not as dramatically as I was, at least not yet.

I had heard and believed so many lies for so long, when I heard something true, it was clear as a bell ringing in my ears. Jesus was real. He died on that cross for all of us broken, sinful people. For me. Jesus was for me, and then He rose from the grave for me. To heal me, to save me, to free me. Jesus was for me, and from that day, I was for Him. There was my forgiveness, there was the savior I had long sought, there was my peace.

I began to search for this program on the TV and listened to every word the preacher had to say; I even began taking notes. I began to read the Bible, not quite grasping all that I read, but learning little by little. I read it from cover to cover as if I had been starving for it, then started all over again. I'd read a selection from the Old Testament, a Psalm and a chapter from Proverbs, then a selection from the New Testament. I devoured other books on Jesus and Christianity and in 1995, even started journaling my thoughts and prayers.

Learning what the Bible had to say was changing me. I had long since lost respect for myself, and now I was finding it again. I remembered all those times God had answered my prayers when we'd gotten ourselves into some scrape or another or had put ourselves into some life-threatening situation. Not to mention the times He had just saved us outright, even when I didn't have sense enough to pray. He never gave up on me.

Although I had read the Bible before, now when I read it, the words came off the page. I understood so much more about God and myself. If I hadn't known what God said, I would have been easily swayed to believe many offbeat religions. Christianity was no longer religion, it was a real relationship with the living God.

Even more than that, I realized I was so valuable to God that He waited patiently for me during all the years I lived so far away from Him. I had made so many bad choices, taken enough drugs to choke a horse, broken the law in a million ways, all the while taking God completely for granted. And still He made sure I finally heard His message of love, redemption and acceptance. I read this in the Bible: "But God demonstrates His own love for us in that while we were yet sinners, Christ died for us." (Romans 5:8 NASB) Who knew!

It just blew me away every time I thought of it back then. It still does to this day.

I became aware that I was changing. I wasn't trying to change; it just happened as I lived my life from day to day. I knew I had been set free from the person I was before. I was a new person and was continually becoming a new person in new ways. I spent more and more time outside during the day and working as much as I could. I stashed away my tip money whenever I could.

Slowly, I was losing my fear and need to appease John and Rachel. I became stronger. I gave up drugs and avoided getting involved in the drug dealing. Living without a drug-induced brain buzz was amazing.

John was losing control of me and he knew it. Trying to keep me in my place, he responded by offering both drugs and sex in more abundance than he ever had. It was almost amusing. Then he decided that we would start having our own church on Sunday mornings. We all sat in a circle in the front room. John would read a passage from the Bible and then we would sing hymns that Lavina had learned from going to church with a friend. I wanted to believe it was sincere, but I knew it was really just a show for my benefit. It didn't last long. But the changes in me did last.

The changes were slow, but steadily real. I questioned more and more whether our lifestyle was what God wanted for me. I began to see that God's way for His people to live was not the life I was living. God wants us to keep sex in marriage and John and I were not married. In fact, sex with John amounted to adultery since he was married to Rachel! It was easy enough to avoid having sex with John – he didn't have time for me anyway. At one point, I moved out of our bedroom. It felt so foreign and it was really confusing the children so I moved back in but slept in a separate bed. I'm sure they thought I was losing my mind.

One day, I asked John about us and if he thought our relationship was biblical. He rambled on hollowly about David, Solomon, Jacob and other men in the Old Testament who had multiple wives and concubines. I asked if he considered me to be his wife. He answered that I was more of a concubine. It's almost impossible for me to describe what washed through me when he said this. I was stunned with a shame and pain and worthlessness I'd never experienced in my life. I felt like a hot knife had been stuck into my heart and burned all the way through to my soul. He said it and just walked away. What a fool I had been! After twenty years and four children together, I realized I was no more than a piece of meat to him.

I had to wonder if he had ever loved me at all and began to question why I believed I loved him. All of this was not love. I knew that because I had experienced real love – the love of Jesus. The underpinnings of the life I'd chosen were melting away. I was starting to get answers about why, many of which were hard to face, even though I knew they were true. I had made my bed and now I realized it was no bed at all – it was a death trap. I also knew I was immensely valuable to the God of the universe, and the knowledge of that kept me sane over the next few years.

It took me awhile to develop the ability to seek and find a life based on the truth, peace and joy that life with Jesus offered.

Chapter 17
Life Goes On. And On. And On

I was being transformed, no question. Yet all the while our lives went on as if nothing had changed one bit. Too often, my response to events reflected hardly any change at all. Rocky had graduated from college and soon married Carla. They had good jobs, a nice home and were very happy. They still are. Lavina started going out with Tony. He had already been busted for drugs and spent time in jail, and now had a pot-growing business with a buddy. He was one cautious guy but let his guard down a bit when he let Lavina's family into his life.

It wasn't long before he and Lavina were engaged, pregnant and living in the cabin on our property. They were married in January, 1994, in Lake Tahoe. Tony was also quite a successful gambler. He paid for everything connected to the wedding with his gambling winnings, and we enjoyed complimentary rooms and meals. Snow and Sonny were home taking care of the house and the animals, and June, who was eight, was staying with a best friend. We got snowed in and stayed a couple of extra days. I hadn't been apart from June that long before, which made me antsy, but we did have a fun time.

Lavina and Tony lived in the cabin until the baby was born. Lavina planned for a home birth, with me and Rachel in attendance. Everything was moving along fine until I realized it was a breach birth. I had read about breach births but wasn't willing to take the risk of handling it correctly, so called a nurse who lived nearby. Unknown to us, she called the fire department and soon an ambulance and paramedics were on the way.

Tony and John had to scramble to hide all the pot before they arrived. Lavina was really close to giving birth. Turns out it was a frank breach – butt first, which I could have managed; a feet-first breach is the one that's not manageable. The ambulance took her to the firehouse, where they transferred her to a helicopter to take her to the hospital about 25 miles north. We then found out it was too foggy to go there, so they were taking her to a valley hospital about 50 miles away.

We got there just as they were taking Lavina in for a C-section. Soon after, they brought beautiful, newborn, black-haired Tina out to her father. So, on August 30, 1994, I became a grandma for the first time! It was also Rachel's birthday – reasons to celebrate all around.

We made a place for them in the house while Lavina recuperated. They moved back to the cabin until it got too cold and then they returned to the house. Things got pretty crowded. They used the front room for their bedroom Snow and June shared the bedroom over the kitchen. I managed to fix (if you want to call it that) the floor in the downstairs apartment to make Sonny a bedroom. We were using the bedroom on the main floor for a silver shop.

The following Thanksgiving, I planned a big dinner. Lavina and Tony were going to look at an 80-acre property located on the Eel River, way up in the hills about 75 miles east. John and Rachel went with them, leaving me with the other kids, preparing dinner. They promised to be back in time for dinner. I cooked and baked and cleaned, set a beautiful table and then waited. It got late. The kids got hungry, so I fed them.

They finally showed up hours later. Not one word was said about the Thanksgiving meal I had prepared for everyone. I had to pretend I wasn't hurt and to be interested in the property and their day's adventure. But I was dying inside. One more time, I tried not to be bitter about being blown off like so much chaff. I had to swallow my tears, I couldn't show any weakness.

In the months since John had told me I was his concubine, I had struggled with a growing hatred for him and Rachel. Every day it welled up inside me and it took a lot of effort on my part to shake it off. Sometimes it came out in how I responded to them, which only made them really angry at me. I had to keep my emotions under control if I wanted to stay there with my children. It was eating me up inside, to the point I couldn't eat anything without experiencing serious pain. I was developing an ulcer – my stuffed emotions were burning up my stomach.

Something had to change, and it did, but it came slowly. Learning to stand up for myself was excruciating. I didn't know how to do it, had no good concept of boundaries, and my concerns about my children complicated things even more. I wasn't sold on taking them away from their father. Yet I was afraid of losing them altogether if I tried. It was very hard to let go of the dream we were supposedly pursuing, and I still believed I could show John and Rachel what a real family could be. God worked with me patiently and lovingly.

Christmas came just after the first pot harvest. It was meager, but we made a lot of money trimming buds for Tony and his partner. John decided to buy an old Cadillac for sale in the valley. We also paid some of the bills but ignored others to buy toys for ourselves and the kids.

Tina was a joy to be around. As grandparents, we got to babysit her often. Lavina was pregnant again before Tina's first birthday. She didn't want to have another C-section so chose to go to an OB-GYN. This was a huge relief to me. I knew my babies' births went smoothly by the grace of God and I wanted the same for Lavina. Little Tony, Jr., was born on April Fool's day in 1995. I was there and all went well with no C-section. Those two grandchildren were and are a great joy in my life. Lavina and Tony had purchased the Eel River property and moved in after Tony, Jr., was born. We called it the 80-Acre Wood.

We were finally getting our jewelry business, The Silver Horse Trading Company, off the ground over that winter. That meant John and Rachel participated in many arts and crafts shows, travelling much of the time. Sometimes they would be gone for a week, return for a couple of days, and then hit the road again. They attended shows up and down the coast, and once even took part in the Rock and Gem Show in Tucson.

I took advantage of some free instruction on making a business plan and securing financing for the business. John let me do this but fought me the whole way. I don't know what he had against being legal; I guess he was still against anything that was straight. Anyway, we obtained a business license and paid taxes.

They were making a lot of good contacts and our unique style of jewelry was becoming known in the arts and crafts world. My job kept me close to home, but when possible, Snow, Sonny and June went along on the trips. It seemed to me that we were finally on our way to success and self-sufficiency through jewelry-making, but the lure of big money in pot-growing made it a mere sideline. We were living off the land alright, just not in the way I had envisioned it all those years earlier.

The pot-growing business is very lucrative – and very hard work. The cultivation work is hard, naturally; but you have to work just as hard to hide what you are doing. The 80-Acre Wood was a very suitable location, remote and with a nearby water source. Just as when we grew the pot in north Georgia for Axle, getting the water to the plants was tough manual labor, carrying the water and walking long distances, often uphill. There was danger on the ground from animals and from people discovering our crop, and from the air, with the authorities in aircraft looking for pot fields. After all, pot-growing was illegal!

Unlike our deal with Axle, John became a full partner in Tony's business. He and Rachel ended up doing a lot of the work because we had very little start-up capital. They spent weeks away working on the property, and when the kids were out of school for the summer, they spent a great deal of time there, as well. Yes, we involved our kids in our pot-growing venture. That left me at home taking care of the house, the animals and working. Communication was sparse because cell phones weren't widely used then, so I only got a call if someone was in town to get supplies.

All went well with our first crop. As I recall, we netted more money than I had ever seen in our 20 years together. Even so, not all the bills got paid. I was doing pretty well with the utilities, car payments and providing for the animals, but we were behind on mortgage payments. It was like pulling teeth to get John to fork out the money to get it caught up. He preferred to use most of the money for his pleasure and to buy jewelry supplies. As usual, I didn't dare to share my opinion of where the money should go. In my skewed thinking, I wasn't the one who put in all the work, so I got no say. I knew that was the answer I'd get from John anyway, served up with his – and Rachel's – anger and harassment. So, not a word. To top it off, John took Rachel to Reno to celebrate her birthday. While I stayed at home.

Snow turned 18 that year. We allowed her to go to dance clubs in Reno, sending Ray with her for protection – a deal he was less than thrilled with

153

since he was too young to go into the clubs. She made lots of friends in the clubs and enjoyed lots of partying. She also started a dating relationship with one of the guys she met. They kept in touch by phone, and he even came to visit her at our home. I wasn't very keen on how their relationship was taking shape.

A few months later, she made plans to travel to Santa Rosa with her boyfriend along with one of her girlfriends and his cousin. A couple of months later – surprise! – she was pregnant. I was devastated by the news. And somehow, Rachel knew before I did! To add to the surprise, the baby's father was the boyfriend's cousin, not the boyfriend. Rachel used the situation to her mock me in her best condescending style, using words like "your daughter" and "her black baby." The overall point was to make it all my fault – you know, like mother, like daughter, sleeping around. As if sexual exploits were something rarely known in our lives.

I think I was in such shock I was not able to respond to her taunting words. As if dealing with her or John's manipulations was something I was able to do even on a good day. Snow tried to stay in touch with the baby's father, but he didn't respond much. They saw each other only one time while she was pregnant. I think he tried to make it clear he didn't want anything to do with the baby or her, but she wasn't getting the message. Like mother, like daughter.

John decided we should all go to Reno for Christmas. We got off to a bad start for a very familiar reason – car trouble. We limped our way along for about 50 miles, then took the car in to a dealer in Ukiah which caused a long delay. So, Lavina and Tony, their kids and Snow got to Reno ahead of us and were already checked into a suite when we got there. Two double rooms were ready for the rest of us. Tony was winning big, which got us the rooms and meals free. I did some gambling and won a little, then lost it all. Tony subsequently lost big, too.

Christmas in Reno just wasn't very Christmas-y. Snow tried several times to meet up with her baby's father, but he never showed. The kids had fun shopping the malls and playing in the video game room. I tried to go with the flow but was not having all that much fun. When we were getting ready to leave the day after New Year's, Snow went into labor; she was about 8-1/2 months along. I wanted to get her home to the hospital where she had pre-arranged to have the baby. But, she was determined to stay in Reno, probably in hopes the father might come to support her and see his baby. Of course, that never happened.

I was with Snow for the whole delivery. In my opinion, there was too much unnecessary drama;

Snow and the baby were doing fine, but the doctor kept intervening in the process. Then, when the baby was born, she looked ashen. The medical staff interpreted her color as blue, never considering she might be biracial, so they whisked her off to an incubator. They only let Snow see and hold her first because I yelled at the nurse. Snow and the baby were released after about three days; and I was glad to leave and thrilled to be back home. So, with all that, Marie – a beautiful little girl – arrived as our third grandchild. Snow was only 19, but she was a great mom and always took very good care of Marie.

Chapter 18
Going … Going …

Our pot-growing business promised to expand when John teamed up with one of our neighbors, Ken, to start raising hydroponically grown pot. Their relationship immediately began to go downhill, which led to John deciding he didn't want to live in California anymore. So, after living in our "crazy house" for 11 years, we put it up for sale. We had never lived anywhere else nearly that long – long enough for all our kids except June to graduate from high school. Amazing! In the next few years, John and Ken's relationship was not all that went downhill.

I was absolutely sure that leaving California was not what I wanted or believed was the right thing to do; I even spoke out clearly against it. John tried to convince me that it was the best thing we could do, but I never agreed with him. June needed to finish school and all her friends were there. I could hardly think of leaving the gardens and orchards that I had worked so hard on and I still believed we could do so much with the potential the property had. Not to mention that my instincts told me the property was going to be worth much, much more in a few years. Turns out, I was right as rain – it is now worth about 6X what we paid for it!

I was aware we had been living in a fish bowl he past 11 years; everyone in the area knew about us – our lifestyle, the drugs, the pot-growing. Sure, this was California with its "anything goes" attitude, but we were still of interest to our neighbors and it made me self-conscious. I couldn't imagine how the kids felt. Still, I did not want to move. I loved our animals and the gardens and wouldn't be able to take them with me to Florida. True to 25 years of how things went down with us, my opinion didn't count for much and I ended up going along with the decision. Florida it was.

A few people showed interest in the house, but no one made a decent offer – mostly, they just wanted something for nothing. Finally, Ken proposed that he would lease the property from us with an option to buy in a year. So that was that. We drew up a contract and had it notarized. We started preparing to move all the way across the country, from northern California to southernmost Florida. We sold everything that was worth something. My Troy-Bilt® tiller was one of the first of my treasures to go. We had purchased a steel building by mail order, which we never even put together; it sold easily. We sold all of our horses, our diesel truck, the horse trailer and much more.

I boxed up the things I wanted to keep, books and so forth, to be shipped to the Keys later. Then John decided I should go to the Keys with the money to purchase a mobile home in Key West. I stayed with our friends Luis and Mary while I searched for a mobile home. I looked at quite a few models, but most were out of our price range or too small. Finally, one came on the market just a few doors down from our friends. It was nicer than most I'd seen, but only single-wide with two bedrooms. I had seen enough to realize I likely wasn't going to do any better, and time was running out. Based on that, I made a deal with the owner to give him part down and the rest when I returned to move in. I returned home to finish packing and get our things ready to ship.

While I was in Florida, Rachel had sold or given away most of my winter clothes, even my favorite leather coat. I felt violated. Who was she to decide what I did or didn't need – not to mention want. It just never stopped. At best, she was just thoughtless – but I suspected she really did things like this just to get under my skin. Mean-spirited.

As soon as school was out for the summer, Snow, Marie, June and I flew to Key West to move into the new home while the rest of the family finished the growing season. We had no car, so we looked

159

for jobs within walking or biking distance. Luckily for me, that meant I got my old job back at the Holiday Inn. Later, I decided to try a new line of work at a small grocery store, in the produce department. I got plenty of exercise biking back and forth to work and everywhere else.

Snow took a telemarketing job to which she either walked or rollerbladed. We worked opposite hours so that Marie was taken care of. June started middle school in Key West. All this was working along really well, except that I was not able to make good on the remaining payment on the mobile home. I had to stall the owner until the crop in California sold.

Lavina and her two kids arrived in September and rented a home on Cudjoe Key, about 25 miles from Key West. Hurricane Irene hit us that fall, and we decided to ride it out in the trailer. The winds weren't too bad, but the flooding came up to the third of five steps to the door. Sea water ruined anything that was not on ground level, but we were spared.

John and Rachel were delayed in coming, so the money we promised to pay for the mobile home was also delayed. John decided we should cut our losses and rent a house up the keys, closer to Lavina, Tony and the kids. Classic John methodology. So, once again we left a burning bridge behind us and moved everything into a rental on Big Pine Key. And once again, I had precious little choice in the matter because I had no control over the money that was supposed to pay for what I had signed for.

John and Rachel said they would send money a little at a time, enough to pay for the rental. I found another job cleaning post offices three days a week. Snow commuted to her new job at a collection agency with a car I rented. I registered June in Marathon Middle School. Seems the rest of us paid the price for John's decisions in chaos, turmoil and working our tails off.

Now that I was apart from John and Rachel, I began to delve more deeply into the Bible and pray about my situation. They were still calling the shots but I had been learning from sermons and Bible teaching on TV and knew my next step of faith was to get involved with other Christian believers. I took a deep breath and went for it.

I looked in the good old Yellow Pages for a church and decided on a non-denominational church – The Vineyard Church. I was quite fearful about this bold step I was about to take. The congregation met in a Quonset hut building. I always went alone and didn't tell anyone where I was going. The people welcomed me at the door. The atmosphere was very informal. The "pews" were just folding chairs set up in front of a stage. There was a band that played lively Christian music, with the words displayed on a screen above the stage so everyone could sing along. The pastor, Steve, was part of the band.

Tables and chairs were placed at the back with coffee and pastries available so you could sit there during the sermon. Everyone was casually dressed – even the pastor wore shorts, sandals and a Hawaiian shirt! At one point, Pastor Steve sat on a stool in front of the stage, played his guitar and sang a song, and then invited the children up and talked to them. After reciting a Bible verse from memory, they were each given a prize and dismissed to Sunday school.

I no longer remember Pastor Steve's sermon that first Sunday, but as I listened I watched the people around me. They were joyful, they had their Bibles open, they were attentive and they were learning. It was great. At one-point Pastor Steve asked people to raise their hand if they saw their need for Jesus and wanted to ask Him to be their Savior. I closed my eyes and slowly raised my hand – not too high – and then I put it back down again quickly. Someone came over to me and gave me a packet of reading material and prayed with me. Yes, I had made this decision a few years back, but not in public and among other believers. It was an amazing feeling and somehow solidified it all for me. There was no way I would ever go back.

The service and worship time were so different from my Catholic church experience I hardly knew what to think. I was surprised, but relaxed and felt so welcome as everyone introduced themselves and shook hands. After attending for a while, I realized this was real church. Warm, welcoming, focused on Jesus, God's Word, and one another. I knew I was part of the family of God, a child of God, with brothers and sisters in Jesus all around me. I knew that nothing could ever take this away from me, and I still know it today. Talk about life-changing! It says in Romans 8, that nothing can separate us from the love of God in Christ Jesus.

Soon John began shipping cars and a boat to Florida. He packed the vehicles with other possessions and put them on an auto transport rig. It had to have cost thousands of dollars. When the vehicles arrived, I was shocked to find out what he had spent all that money on. The cars were at least 20 years old – a Jaguar, a Lincoln Mark III limited edition, and a Lincoln limousine – and each one needed plenty of work to get them running. The boat was nice, and large – but its engine wasn't suitable for salt water! In other words, it was all a big waste.

Just after Thanksgiving, John and Rachel finally finished their business and joined us in the Keys; our son Sonny came with them. The house next door came up for rent, so we rented that to accommodate everyone. It was also a welcome

163

chance for me to live separately a while longer, making it much easier to follow my new life. I attended church whenever John and Rachel were not around; I knew they would belittle and discourage me if they knew what I was doing.

In the evenings, they went Christmas shopping for trees, decorations and gifts, spending money like there was no tomorrow. They were both so strung out when they arrived in Florida that they spent most of the daytime inside a dark room, smoking opium almost nonstop to keep the DT's away. It was really heartbreaking to watch our son go through this also. They ran out of drugs and became sick with vomiting and chills until they reunited with old friends in Key West. That got them back into the whole party and cocaine scene. Most everything they did occurred in the dark. They stayed out until dawn, wheeling and dealing drugs, then returning to sleep all day until it was time to get up and do it all again.

I usually bowed out by volunteering to stay with the kids. Every now and then, I'd feel left out and join in, only to soon be sorry I went along. I came to understand that as a Jesus follower, the Holy Spirit was living in me and letting me know when I'd made the wrong choice. But even as He corrected me, His love for me was clear, tender and powerful.

Lavina, Tony, Snow and Sonny got involved in the drug scene along with John and Rachel. By Christmas, every one of them was badly strung out. Sonny got quite sick and, I think, was ready to call it quits but was always pulled back into it due to intimidation from his dad. If you weren't doing what John was doing, that meant you were against him. This is when our relationship really began to rip apart.

I believe John began to deeply distrust me and question my loyalty to our family, especially when I thwarted his affections. We had been separated by time and miles for months, and emotionally for much longer than that. I was leaning more toward living for Jesus every day and John was headed in another direction. I was still such a new Christian that I didn't fully grasp the power Jesus could have in totally transforming a life.

I was caught in a crazy web. On the one hand, I knew beyond a doubt that I wanted to follow Jesus. His love for me was inescapable; there was nothing else like it. The relationships I was developing with other believers were amazing. On the other hand, there was John. He still had a strong hold on me. No, the constraints weren't physical. But they were real. He, Rachel and I had been together for 25 years. He was the father of my children. As up, down, and all around as it had been, it was our life. My life. I couldn't begin to imagine another life might be out there for me.

165

Yet, I had spent years feeling unappreciated and insignificant. I remember one night I proudly brought home $300 in tips. John's response? He just wanted me to give it to him so he could buy more dope. No words of praise, no words of thanks. I didn't matter and I was never good enough. Yes, I had moved away emotionally to some degree, but I didn't yet know how to break away completely.

But it was coming.

Chapter 19
Gone

Just after the start of the new year, the lease was up on both of our houses. Of course, I was the one who had to go and find a new place to live because they were the ones who had done all the hard work for the money. They climbed up the steep hillsides almost every day, hauled the water, carried the harvest out, and then did all the trimming, packaging and selling. Anything I had done didn't count since they brought in the big bucks. That was what really counted.

The new rental home was located on Big Pine Key. It was a much bigger home on a canal, and quite nice. In addition to all of us, we had our dachshunds, Frank and Mary Jane. We had been breeding, raising and selling the pups for a year or two. I took care of the papers, vet visits and so forth. That was my assignment since I was considered not talented enough to be in our jewelry-making business. Actually, I'm thankful that God kept me out of the other business, especially since it became the only business.

In order for the landlord to accept our application, I had to lie about how many people were going to be living there, and about the presence of the dogs. I was never able to relax, fearing the real estate company would find out and I would be held totally responsible (which I was) because I had signed the contract. I was sure the police would show up at the door at any moment. Our neighbors were friends with the owner and watched our every move while we lived there.

After getting settled there, we began house-hunting, looking to buy a home of our own. To my thinking, the ones we were looking at would get us in way over our heads. We found a nice older home on a canal with an in-ground swimming pool; it was located on a double lot just around the corner from the rental. It was the house John wanted to have.

We began the negotiations with the owner, getting the inspection and hammering out a deal. We agreed we'd pay half of the down payment now and the other half in 6 months. Little did the owner know that meant John and Rachel had to return to California to sell the rest of the pot they had hidden away.

I was included because I could do all the work. I handled the negotiations with the real estate and loan companies. To provide proof of income, I used the jewelry business as the source and made up sales documents and receipts. As it turned out, I didn't get to sign the contract. At this point, I had bad credit and John and Rachel had no credit.

168

God has such a sense of humor. He didn't let me get away with my old tricks this time. No cheating, no lying. I don't know why I continued to do John and Rachel's bidding; I suppose it was for the kids. They needed a home and I was tired of moving. Deep down, I figured I deserved something too.

As soon as John and Rachel returned with the down payment, the paperwork was signed and we were cleared to move in. It was February. Somehow, I ended up doing most of the moving myself. I was anxious to be out of the rental before the owner came to inspect it. Somehow during the move, I lost a Star quilt that Rachel had made. I'm not sure what happened to it; I figure it got piled with the bedding that belonged with the house when I did the laundry. I was accused of doing it on purpose. Just one more black mark against me.

By the end of April, John, Rachel and Tony went back to California to start the next crop. John forced Sonny to go along, even though he was content right where he was. He liked his job and was dating a cute girl, so he did not want to leave. But, you didn't say no to John. We were short on funds again, so to get their plane tickets for California, I pawned the diamond earrings John had given me as Christmas gift years before.

After they left I no longer had to fear their ridicule when I went to church on Sundays and Bible study

169

on Wednesday nights. This was my first experience with a Bible study. I enjoyed learning and being with other Christians and loved my freedom. June started attending church with me and eventually, Snow and Marie did, too.

Life began to seem normal for the first time in a long time. Lavina and the kids remained in Florida while Tony was in California. I enjoyed opportunities to babysit and taking care of Marie while Snow worked. June became best friends with a girl she met at school. She encouraged June to join the swim team. June soon got into good shape because they practiced every day and competed in swim meets.

Then the bottom dropped out. The rest of the world was safely into Y2K, but we were in serious trouble. John, Tony and Rachel were busted. The District Attorney in Sacramento County had decided to make an example of John and Tony since they had been growing pot on Federal land. Plus, each already had two strikes against them per California law. Tony had two drug charges pertaining to growing and possession from a few years earlier, and John had drug possession and selling charges from when he was younger. They were arrested and remained in the Sacramento County jail for almost two years awaiting trial.

During the first few months John was able to call us once or twice a week to give us instructions on

170

what he wanted us to do. Lavina returned to California with her kids so she could sell their property and get some money together for Tony's lawyer. They met up with Rachel and stayed with her family until the first of the year.

Things continued to unravel. Ken, John's former business partner, decided he wasn't going to pay his rent on our Albion house anymore. Seems he was thinking he and his wife could somehow just take the property from us since John was now in jail. In fact, we had suspicions he was the one who called in the tip that got John and Tony arrested. No one else really knew what they were doing or where to find them. We needed that rent money to pay the mortgage on our present home. I finally had to get the sheriff to evict Ken and his family. We put the property up for sale.

Lavina found a buyer for the 80-Acre Wood and made a deal with them. All this took time, and the more time that went by, the further behind we got on our mortgage, and there was a balloon payment looming. I took a second job with a small company cleaning vacation rentals; the work was sporadic but paid really well. Snow worked with me when she could. The owner wanted me to buy the business, but I wasn't ready to take that on.

That job led to working with a real estate rental company. It paid well and I didn't have to give up cleaning the post offices. Finally, I started cleaning as an independent contractor, and got a second job in a grocery store. Snow started working for an art dealer in hopes of making large commissions. She also spent her nights going out with her friends, drinking and smoking pot. June did a lot of babysitting, and I became the main caregiver for Marie.

Lavina, the kids and Rachel returned to Florida to ride out the winter. We all stayed in the house. Things began to get pretty tense. All this time Sonny had been hiding from California authorities. We talked to him occasionally but had to use pay phones so the calls couldn't be traced. We were pretty sure we were all being watched.

Lavina took a job as a waitress/bartender at night. After work, she would go out with her girlfriend until the wee hours of the morning while I looked after the children. Rachel didn't do anything except take pills and sleep. Tina was four and Tony Jr. was three. They were completely undisciplined, without regular mealtimes or bedtimes. They had dark circles under their eyes from too little sleep and too much television. I started to get them into a routine, but it was a struggle, neither Rachel or Lavina seem to care how the children behaved.

The time came for Lavina and Rachel to return to California to see John and Tony and to finish up selling the properties. This time, they left the

172

children with me and Snow. They were gone six weeks. Snow and I juggled our schedules to be sure the kids were taken care of and struggled to pay the bills, but by the grace of God we managed to make it through.

All the while John was calling from jail to give us our to do list. He seemed convinced we were slackers and absolutely sure we were partying his money away. What a joke! He didn't see that with Lavina and Rachel gone, there was only me and Snow to keep food in the cabinets and a roof over our heads. The mortgage payment on the new house was way out of our range, and the inefficient air conditioners were eating us alive in electricity bills. We couldn't begin to afford to pay someone to take care of the pool, and my efforts to do it were useless. So, we couldn't use the pool. It was a good thing the kids got me a lawn mower for my birthday – at least I could keep the yard looking presentable!

The house needed some minor and major repairs that I couldn't handle. John finally gave us permission to sell the boat, the Jaguar and the Lincoln limo. It took a while but finally the boat sold for a few hundred dollars. You know, the boat that couldn't be used in the salt water that was all around us. We also got a buyer for the limo, which wouldn't start, so it sold for a song. That money evaporated pretty quickly after we paid a round of bills. I put the Jaguar on eBay thinking it would

173

surely sell since it was an old classic. No such luck. Things were looking pretty bleak. Snow and I continued to bust our tails to hold things together and John continued to complain and give orders.

One Saturday I was on the internet trying to sell the Jaguar. Snow was in her room getting dressed and the kids were outside playing. Little Tony came in and was trying to tell me something. I was focused on the computer and only half listening. He was persistent and kept pointing out to the canal. Finally, I got up and followed him outside only to see Marie floating face down in the canal. I jumped in and swam to her as she was rolling over on her back, floating down the canal.

When I got to her, she was breathing so I swam back to our dock with her in tow. Little Tony and Tina were watching all this from the edge of the dock. I yelled for Tina to go get Snow. She came out and pulled Marie out of the water. Praise God, she was alright! A little shaken, of course, but had not swallowed much water. We had been teaching all the kids to swim so she knew to hold her breath when she turned over in the water. That, plus the fact she was in salt water, kept her afloat and alive. About an hour later, we were all at the Flea Market as if nothing had happened. Once again, God was right there.

We told no one about that scare until Lavina and Rachel returned about a week later. We learned

174

that Rachel was scheduled to turn herself in to the police in California and was going to spend a year in jail for her part in the pot business. They also told us that Sonny now had a warrant out for his arrest. Trouble, trouble, and more trouble. With even more to come.

Rachel had immediately passed on to John the story of Marie's near drowning. To punish me, he stopped calling. Little did he realize it was probably the best favor he ever did for me. He was calling Rachel instead. She had decided to live with Lavina in another rental, mostly because she thought I was not doing her bidding as she expected. Little did she realize that she too had done me the favor of a lifetime. I was finally over cowering before her and waiting on her hand and foot. She didn't appreciate it; anyway, she and Lavina were pretty strung out on cocaine and pills, so they belonged together.

John wasn't calling me, but he did write me an eight-page letter. He was livid because I did not tell him about Marie being in the canal – as if he was in a position to do anything about it. He ranted about everything, including my going to church, being a hypocrite, a lousy mother and grandmother, not working hard enough to pay the bills, spending all his money, disrespecting Rachel and kicking her out of his house. His house?

As usual, I could do nothing right, Rachel could do nothing wrong, and Snow – his own daughter – was no good. He also intimated that Snow and I were the ones who turned him and Tony in to the police. He wanted me and Snow out of his house ASAP. This was the last straw for me. I was devastated. After being loyal to him and to Rachel for 25+ years! I gave them everything and treated them like gold. I had his babies, worked and gave him all my money, held things together for them. All I could do was walk around the house aimlessly for hours, crying and cursing and reading the letter over and over.

Finally, I just gave up and turned every bit of it over to God. It was beyond me to handle it. Far, far beyond me. I fasted for three days, praying about all of it. Then I decided to call my brother. He told me it was time to leave and would send plane tickets for me and June to come to Ohio. Snow didn't want to leave. I packed up everything that was mine and moved it all to a storage locker, then packed the clothes June and I needed. We left a month before school was out.

I rented a car to drive to the Fort Lauderdale airport. On the way out of the Keys, we stopped by Lavina's to say goodbye to her and the kids. Rachel cornered me outside and tried to get me to leave June behind. When she realized I was not backing down to her will, she became like another person, almost hissing at me. Sneering, she told me to go ahead and visit my family, but I had better return or send June back to live in Florida. I knew she didn't care whether I came back or not. I felt as if I was in the presence of pure evil. I left with June and we fled to my family in Ohio. I needed a place of grace.

Chapter 20
And So, I Have

Once in Ohio, June and I stayed at my youngest sister's home for a few weeks but it was tense and uncomfortable. I couldn't pinpoint the reason but had to wonder if it was because we were crowded; my mother was also living there. Later it came to light that my brother-in-law was seeing another woman. He eventually left my sister and asked for a divorce. We then went to live with my older sister. June and I shared a small bedroom. I slept on an air mattress on the floor and let June sleep on the single bed.

June was getting bored and wanted to go back to Florida to see her friends. To get her mind on something else, I had her finish the school year with her cousin so she could meet kids her age and spend time with them. Finally, it came time to decide whether to return to Florida or stay in Ohio. My mother said if I stayed, she would buy me a car and if I went back, she would give me the money to rent a place for June and myself to live on our own.

It was a difficult, difficult decision. I researched Key West rentals on the internet and prayed a lot. In the end, I couldn't bring myself to go back. Yet, I thought I'd consider it once Rachel had gone to jail. Meanwhile, June was not doing well; her hair was falling out and she couldn't sleep or eat. I was worried. We took her to the doctor. It wasn't a surprise to find out she didn't have a physical illness. She was in shock over the separation – from her dad, her home, her siblings, her school and her best friend. With the help of her cousin, she gradually improved and became herself again. She and her cousin had a lot in common as her father was also incarcerated. She had been through a lot, too.

John and Tony were each found guilty and sentenced to 10 years in prison. Rachel was also found guilty of conspiracy and was sentenced to one year.

I ultimately made the decision to stay in Ohio and away from John and Rachel. There were times I wish I had gone back because I missed Snow, Sonny, Lavina and my grandchildren so painfully. But I just couldn't do it. I had a lot of adjusting to go through but I made progress day by day. My mother, brothers and sisters had been praying for me for many years, along with a host of others in my brother's church. They'd never even met me! Unconditional love makes all the difference.

The Albion house finally sold, Lavina found a buyer who was willing to pay $250,000 for it. I was communicating with the lawyer who was handling the sale and was trying to get a share of the money. I thought I deserved one-third or even one-half of the profit. John and Rachel wanted me to have nothing. I got tired of fighting them and settled for $2000. Enough for June and me to move into our own place. I needed a clean break from all my past.

I thought a lot about why it took me so long to break away. I know now it was only with Jesus that I had the strength and the courage to leave and then to stay away and start a new life. God has never once stopped looking out for me, from the night I put my broken rosary under my pillow to this very day. I have come to better understand what Paul when he wrote, "Therefore we do not lose heart, but though our outer man is decaying, yet our inner man is being renewed day by day." (2 Corinthians 4:16 NASB). That was it, I was and am still being renewed day by day.

I have found a place of grace. I have built a new life. I have a wonderful relationship with my siblings and extended family, although my oldest brother passed away in 2004 and my sweet mother in 2006. I am so blessed that I was able to spend five precious years reunited with them. I married a man I met after I moved back to Ohio; he passed away in 2008. My church family has loved me and supported me through every joy and sorrow of the past 17 years. For the past few years, I've been living in northern California with my son Sonny, helping him out with his kids. I have a fabulous church family there, too!

My oldest son, Rocky, has been married for 20 years and lives with his wife Carla in the San Francisco Bay area. He teaches high school math and is also an artist. Carla is a librarian. He has little or no contact with his brother or sisters, although not by his choice.

Lavina, my oldest daughter, divorced Tony while he was serving his 10-year sentence for his involvement in the pot business. She has remarried and lives with her two children and second husband in North Carolina. She has also become a Jesus follower, along with her husband. One day while I was having a conversation about Jesus with her two children, they chose to believe in Jesus as their Savior also. Tina recently got her degree in Hospitality and Management and Tony, Jr., Is working as a chef.

My middle daughter Snow has had a hard time over the years. She was involved in an abusive relationship for eight years. Now, though, Snow is making progress toward overcoming all this. She recently moved back to California and is reconnecting with friends from high school. Marie is attending college in Florida.

Sonny, my younger son, turned himself in to California authorities about the time I headed back to Ohio and was sentenced to community service and a year's probation. When he had completed that, he met a girl and married. He and his wife had two children, a boy and a girl. They are now divorced and Sonny has full custody of the kids. He is fully committed to the care of his daughter and autistic son.

June, the baby of the family, is now married and after living in Ohio for 15 years, she and her husband moved to the Bay Area and are thriving.

While Rachel was serving her one year for conspiracy for her part in the pot business, she became a believer in Jesus. She apologized to me and me to her, so our relationship improved. I kept her at arm's length to a certain extent; I had to, little by little, learn to trust her and her motives. She and John divorced in 2016, and she passed away in 2017. Rachel had her faults, but I would be wrong not to point out that when Rachel died, the world lost a uniquely talented artist and craftswoman. She was one of the only surviving Native American Pomo basket weavers. She was also a silversmith, created beautiful leather and beadwork, and incorporated her basket-weaving designs into her jewelry.

I have to say in John's defense that he was charismatic and likable and was often fun to be with. He was also a great hunter and fisherman, providing us with fresh seafood and meat over the years. Our relationship hasn't mended. I have attempted to contact him but he refuses to

182

acknowledge me. He still doesn't see his need for the Savior.

The love of Jesus is very, very powerful. It draws us, as it drew me, out of darkness and into His glorious light. In the midst of all its power, His love is also tender, soothing, unending, and absolutely transformative.

As I spent time in the Bible, I learned that God made us for His glory. Can you imagine that? Me. Made for God's glory! I had taken a path that brought anything but glory to anyone, a path that obscured God from me. But God made sure that my awareness of Him, while obscured, was never obliterated.

He was always right there and involved. To know that, all I have to do is think back about the many prayers He answered through the years. Or the Good Samaritans He sent to rescue us – more than once. And, how He just outright saved the lives of Snow, Marie and June. I gave Him little or no credit then but I sure do now. I brought God into the picture when it suited me, then ignored Him the rest of the time – and all the while, there I was, yearning for a savior.

I chose a life I thought was right and would be fulfilling and worthwhile; a life that would be my salvation, and that of John and Rachel. It's pretty clear now how wrong I was. It's also very clear

183

now that God loved me anyway and right through every dark, twisted, selfish, dangerous and wrong-headed choice I made. He's no puppet-master. He lets us make our choices until we choose our way into a mess bigger than we can deal with. And once we're there, He's there too, ready and waiting to show us the way out. His way. The way that will bring glory to Him. He doesn't wait for us to clean ourselves up. He just takes us right where we are, in all our ugliness. He loves us! That is the definition of grace.

It wasn't so much the nomadic, anti-cultural, drug-laced lifestyle I was part of. All that was just the symptom of the real problem. I was broken and that's how my brokenness expressed itself. According to what God has to say about it, we're all broken. "For all have sinned and fall short of the glory of God." (Romans 3:23 NASB). And our brokenness shows itself in a million different ways.

We go our own way, without considering Him. We think we're fine and it never occurs to us we might be sideways and need to get put right side up. In the midst of it all, God keeps tapping us on the shoulder, tugging at our shirtsleeve, crossing in front of us waving His arms as if to say, "Hey you! I'm over here! You're headed in the wrong direction. Join Me, follow Me and let Me lead you in the way I've chosen for you." He did that with me for years. I finally stopped and listened to Him that day I walked in from the yard, paid attention

and heard the truth about Jesus from that
evangelist on TV.

As I went through my days, I was able to apply
what I was learning, a piece of it here, a piece of it
there, and things started to change. I was set
free. I gained the courage to go against John and
Rachel's flow and go with God's flow. Jesus's love
for me was, and is, so palpable and so real that I
began to choose it above all my fear and
selfishness and hard-headedness. I became a new
person. As the Bible puts it, "Therefore if anyone is
in Christ, he is a new creature; the old things
passed away; behold, new things have come."
(2 Corinthians 5:17 NASB)

I have also learned that whatever names you,
owns you. For thirty years I walked as Serena,
but Jesus gave me the name Marylyn. When He
called me to Himself, I heard an audible voice say
my name. That's when I knew I was created
anew. It almost knocked me over. There have
been a few times I have heard Him call my name,
I knew He was always with me and watching over
me. Zephaniah 3:17 (ESV) says: "The Lord your
God is in your midst, a mighty one who will save:
He will rejoice over you with gladness; He will
quiet you by His love; He will rejoice over you with
loud singing."

There is a story in Luke 7:36-50 in the New Testament that makes me think of what God did for me. Jesus was having dinner at an important Jewish man's house, Simon the Pharisee. A low-life woman, well known for her ugly lifestyle, came into Simon's home and began to clean Jesus's feet with her tears and hair, and applying perfume to them. The man thought arrogantly to himself that if Jesus was really a prophet, He'd know what sort of woman this sinner was.

Jesus then told him a story about two debtors, one of whom owed their lender much more than the other one did. They both were unable to pay their debts, and the lender forgave them both what they owed, no strings. Jesus then asked the Pharisee which of the debtors loved the lender more. The Pharisee answered that he thought it would be the one who owed more.

Jesus told him he was exactly right and reminded him that he neglected to greet Him with a kiss, wash His feet, or anoint His head with oil when He arrived – all typical customs of respect in their culture. Jesus then summed it up this way, "I say to you, her sins, which are many, have been forgiven, for she loved much; but he who is forgiven little, loves little." (v47 NASB) And He told the woman her sins were forgiven.

The passage closes out with Jesus saying to the *woman,* "Your faith has saved you, go in peace." (v50 NASB)

And so, I have.

EPILOGUE

My life has not been ordinary, neither has it been extraordinary; it has just been other. I am not proud of it now, but when I was going through it I had so much pride that it blinded me. I am not a writer and don't aspire to be one but, I needed to write this story down in hopes that it would inspire someone to make changes, and to give hope where there may be none. What I have written is my personal recollection of the events; I have not embellished on the them. I left a lot of the story out because some details would not be appropriate and even hurtful.

There is no denying that I was having fun but at a great cost to me and my children. I had the privilege to learn basket weaving, silversmithing, leatherwork and beadwork from the best.

God is patient.

"It is a trustworthy statement deserving full acceptance, that Christ Jesus came into the world to save sinners, among whom I am foremost of all. Yet for this reason I found mercy, so that in me as the foremost, Jesus Christ might demonstrate His perfect patience as an example for those who would believe in Him for eternal life." (1 Timothy 1:15-16 NASB)

There is a song by the group Selah called "Unredeemed". A few of the lyrics go like this:

"For every choice that led to shame and all the love that never came
For every vow that someone broke and every lie that gave up hope
We live in the shadow of the fall but the cross says these are all
Places where grace is soon to be so amazing
It may be unfulfilled, it may be unrestored
But when anything that's shattered
is laid before the Lord
Just watch and see it will not be unredeemed.

Made in the USA
Lexington, KY
21 June 2018